The Movie Reporter

HOW TO CHOOSE A GOOD VIDEO *EVERY* TIME!

by Phil Boatwright

FEATURES:

Synopsis and content of newly released videos.

Quality Video Alternatives with the same theme or style as the newest releases, but without the abusive language, violence, sexual situations, etc.

Videos you'll enjoy with the little ones.

Inspirational videos available at Christian bookstores.

Studio and network addresses.

And more!

CONTENTS

ISBN 1-55748-267-5

THE MOVIE REPORTER

PRINTED IN THE U.S.A.

FOREWORD

THE PURPOSE OF *THE MOVIE RE-PORTER*

In the '40s, '50s or even the '60s, parents could send their children off to the Saturday matinee with assurance that the movie studios had some regard for taste and temperance. The attitude of the entertainment industry during the '80s, and so far in the '90s, has changed. Now there are no taboos. Anything goes. Exploitive sexuality, brutal violence, liberal doses of profanity and crudity, anti-Christian and Jewish sentiments, controversial political views and a drifting away from traditional family values now present family leaders with a major dilemma, as the Saturday matinee has come into the living room via the video cassette.

The Movie Reporter is a compilation of movies, videos, and articles reviewed and written from a Christian's perspective. It has been designed to give the content of newly released videos in an effort to assist families searching for appropriate movie fare.

The MPAA rating system does not answer all the questions.

Haven't you occasionally been surprised by what you've seen or heard in a PG film? Many people have found objectionable material in G-rated movies. Violence, language and sex are not the only objections many film-goers are finding at the movies. A filmmaker's extreme political and social views may also cause concern for parental figures.

An alternative to political pontification as well as much mediocrity and profane material coming from today's artistic elite, *The Movie Reporter* also presents "Video Alternatives": films with the same theme or style as the new release, but without the objectionable material. Quality pictures are featured—some educational, most edifying, all entertaining.

Also, the book presents many Inspirational Videos available at Christian bookstores, representing most Christian denominations. *The Movie Reporter, How To Choose A Good Video Every Time,* has been developed, not only to make you aware of the product coming from the film industry, but also to give you some options and to let you know how you can most effectively take a stand against pornography, profanity, religion-bashing and violence in movies. Did you know that the television networks consider one letter the equivalent to hearing from 1,000 viewers? The motion picture studios have similar ideas concerning the amount of mail received. But we'll get into that in Chapter VII.

The first question to be addressed is one of the most important and most debated by 20th-century Christian fellowships, SHOULD WE VIEW MOVIES?

Ultimately, that is a decision each of us must make for ourselves. For many Christians, the question isn't, should we view films, but which films should we view? I believe the Bible has an answer to that question. It is found in Philippians 4:8. "Finally, brothers, whatever is true, whatever is noble, whatever is right, whatever is pure, whatever is lovely, whatever is admirable, if anything is excellent or praiseworthy, think about such things." And: "Test everything. Hold on to the good. Avoid every kind of evil" (l Thessalonians 5:21-22). "I will set before my eyes no vile thing" (Psalms 101). "Have no fellowship with the unfruitful works of darkness, but rather reprove them" (Ephesians 5:11).

Even the movies themselves have occasionally expressed enlightenment on the subject: "Your head is like a gas tank. You have to be really careful about what you put in it, because it might just affect the whole system" (from the film *I've Heard the Mermaids Singing*, Miramax Films).

Personally, I've been positively affected by many films. Good story-telling, like the parables taught by our Lord, has greatly influenced my life. I've reasoned that my decisions affect the lives of others (*It's a Wonderful Life*). I've learned to stand up for causes, no matter the outcome (*To Kill a Mockingbird*). I've come to regard others with respect (*Documentary on Mother Teresa*). I've seen that life is a banquet (*Babette's Feast*) and I've tried to take the high-road after viewing Cary Grant and Fred Astaire, ascertaining that class wasn't just knowing which fork to eat with, but also not being judgmental when others didn't.

Viewing motivations on the silver screen has helped me to understand my fellow man. And I believe it is good to be moved emotionally. I've cried and laughed and been nourished by many motion pictures. On the other hand, there is nothing worse than having two hours of your life stolen by deceptive movies, that "take" while maintaining the illusion of "giving" (*Track 29*).

Whether you attend movies or not, the facts are clear: Billions are made each year by the entertainment industry. That means a lot of our countrymen, including Christians, are attending movies on a regular basis. I simply want to apprise them of the content of these pictures, thereby giving them the data to make informed decisions as to the suitability of movies for their families.

In an attempt to motivate other Christians to become involved with needed changes in the motion picture industry, I try to point out the direction Hollywood is taking our society by giving the content (the reason for the rating) of each newly released picture. With offensive elements overriding the content and quality of media presentations, it's important for Christians to be aware and to express their feelings concerning these directions. (Not that we will change the climate of the movie community, but that we can have a positive effect on *some* filmmakers and, therefore, on a portion of society.)

A new morality is clearly existent in our society, but *not all change is progress*. The casual presentation of something anti-moral is abundant in most TV programs and films coming from Hollywood. It has become the norm. So what should we do about it? Being proud that we, ourselves, don't watch television or attend movies is not answer enough.

The first step is to be informed. Since the Motion Picture Association of America's rating system is very vague, there is need for a tool that features movie content—a guide that is unbiased, presenting facts over opinions.

Without "boycotting" anybody or causing war with the members of the motion picture community, *The Movie Reporter* believes that if you have the data, you'll make wise choices about what kind of images you continually put into your mind, and see for yourself the direction Hollywood is leading our society. The motto of *The Movie Reporter Newsletter* is "Know before you go," or, in the case of this book, "Know before you rent."

Thanks to Barbour and Company, Inc. for the faith they've expressed in me.

A very special thank-you to Paragon Word Processing and Terri Nigro for her professionalism and insight.

CHAPTER I

HOLLYWOOD'S MYTH

Violence + Profanity + Nudity = Big Bucks

Recently I viewed *See You In the Morning*, a Warner Brothers release starring Jeff Bridges, Alice Krige and Farrah Fawcett (looking better than ever). It is an excellent picture about the positive aspects of marriage and the devastating consequences of divorce.

This touching comedy will have you laughing and crying and shouldn't be missed by troubled parents considering divorce.

That's the review I'd like to give this video release. Alas, there is an obstacle. Many of our readers will be offended by the few unwarranted expletives sprinkled throughout the film for no other apparent reason than acquiring a PG rating.

The great myth begins with filmmakers prophesying that the general public will not support a G-rated film. My question is, how do they know that? The mainstream movie-makers (other than Disney) haven't made a G-rated film in fifteen years. Are you telling me if you brought together the talents of Streep, Hoffman and Scorsese, people would stay away because the newspaper ads carried a G rating?

I attended the American Film Market last year and each of the twenty films I viewed contained the same three requirements for maintaining the Hollywood myth—bad language, violence, and some degree of nudity.

Perhaps if the Hollywood moguls would replace these prerequisites with talent, taste and creativity, they would find themselves deserving of their titles and possibly gaining our respect.

Hollywood keeps forcing these elements upon the viewing public, yet it is the exceptions such as *Chariots of Fire, Driving Miss Daisy, Awakenings, Henry V, Hamlet, Enchanted April,* and *Beauty and the Beast* that garner our respect and usually the industry's most coveted awards.

Now, if I were to suggest that all films conform to this category, artists would consider that censorship. Arguably, there may be a place for explicit matter, but why should unoffensive films be the minority? After all, adult subjects are generally more profound when handled with discretion.

The silver screen and the "boob tube" are here to stay. Their power dwarfs the strength of all the weapons known to man, because they devastate not the body, but the mind and spirit. So who's going to stand up for quality and decency in the media if not the readers of this book?

Perhaps the duty of the Christian believer is not just to turn off the TV set or refrain from theater-going, but to be aware, to speak up, and most importantly, to be responsible for the images we subject our children to. It's time to take a stand against the great myth.

NC-17, THE NEW AND CONFUSED X-RATING

Give me a break. The only reason for legitimizing an X rating is to allow more extensive coverage of violence and sexual situations. By abolishing the X for the noncommittal NC-17, Hollywood signals the making of more films to fill a category heretofore restrained by theater owners and media advertising departments.

The masked excuse for this new rating? To allow adult subjects to be presented without fear of association with pornography. What's so silly about this subterfuge is that there is no subject under the sun that hasn't been handled within the restraint of the R or even PG-13 rating. (Adult treatments are generally more profound when handled with discretion.)

What promoters of this new rating are really saying is that society wants to see more sex and more controversial brutality. It isn't the "adult" subjects that will gain the NC-17, but rather the presentation of bizarre sexual behavior and explicit violent acts.

STOP PROFANITY IN MOVIES!

Using Christ's name in vain is becoming commonplace in almost every movie. Most filmmakers are simply unaware of how offensive the practice of using God's name in vain really is to Believers.

Just seen a film where Christ's name was used as

an obscene expletive? Do something positive about it.

Write to that filmmaker or studio with Christ's love, letting them know how offensive and unnecessary those profanities are. Pray over that letter and send it today.

Get involved. You can make a difference. Each letter represents the feelings of over 1,000 viewers. Remember, profanity is not only offensive, it's against the law—the third law ever given: "You shall not misuse the name of the Lord your God, for the Lord will not hold anyone guiltless who misuses His name" (Exodus 20:7, NIV).

The addresses of the movie studios, networks, and cable companies are featured in Chapter VII.

DEFINITIONS

Crudity—Lacking in culture, tact

Expletive—An obscene word or phrase

Obscenity—Objectionable or repugnant to acceptable standards of decency or morality; indecent; pornographic; offensive in language or action.

Profanity—Irreverence toward God or holy things.

Blasphemy—To speak impiously or contemptuously of God or sacred things.[1]

Adult Subject Matter—Situations or subjects unsuitable for or difficult to comprehend by children.

CHOOSING A RENTAL VIDEO
(With No More Mistakes)

Has this ever happened to you? You enter a video store, spend twenty minutes walking up and down the aisles, examining one unknown video box after another until, finally, mostly out of exasperation, you pick one, only to discover after ten minutes of viewing at home that it is unsuitable for your family. You checked the rating. You admired the actors. Yet the film was a piece of junk. It's happened to me.

Everybody Wins starred Nick Nolte and Debra

---

[1] All definitions except "Adult Subject Matter" are from *New Webster's Dictionary*.

Winger and was written by Arthur Miller. I thought those were three aces, but the only winners were the folks who missed it.

There are safeguards to alleviate this frustration. Here are a few suggestions.

One, don't rent a video that hasn't got a rating. (Exception: Movies made before the late '60s were governed by a code which forbade objectionable material.) If you want adventure, climb a mountain or go parasailing, but don't rent an unknown movie!

Second, do a little research. Ask qualified people what they thought of a certain film. Don't depend on video store employees to furnish you with specific information. I can't tell you how many times I've overheard a video salesperson recommend a film with some merit, but usually containing very offensive material. Also, many young clerks are unaware of any film not made in the last three months. *Get your information before you enter the video store!*

Third, subscribe to guides such as *The Movie Reporter Newsletter* that present reviews from a Christian perspective. You may not like every film that's been recommended, but at least you won't be in for a hostile surprise. Perceptive readers can get much out of the secular reviewers, but many critics are slack about mentioning promiscuity, profanity or Christian-bashing.

Fourth, look past the "New Arrivals" in the video store. Check out the "Classics" section. Just because a film has some age on it doesn't mean it won't relate. I realize it's difficult to convince young people to view anything made before they were born, but if they will open up to the experience, they will discover some memorable film-making. Come to think of it, the idea bears merit for studio execs as well!

Fifth, before going to the video shop, have a few selections in mind and call around. Most "hard to finds" are worth the effort. Ask the store employee to reserve your choices. Take a few minutes to write in your local video store phone numbers in the front of this book. This may sound like a lot of effort, but actually you'll find yourself saving time and energy.

And last, remember to bring *The Movie Reporter* with you each time you visit the video store. It will help, I promise.

CHAPTER II

NEWLY RELEASED VIDEOS
And Their Video Alternatives

Neither *The Movie Reporter* nor our distributors are recommending newly released movies. This book simply presents the content of each new video for the purpose of assisting you in choosing films appropriate for your family's viewing.

Realizing the newest releases will catch your eye the moment you enter a video store, I acknowledge many of these films so you can be advised as to their content. Take note of the **Video Alternatives.** They feature the same theme or style as the newest releases but lack today's extreme violence, abusive profanity or exploitive sexual situations.

I believe the Video Alternatives to be the most important part of this book. To my knowledge, there is no other publication or film critic presenting such a feature at this time. These Video Alternatives (Vid. Alt.) are considered to be 3- or 4-star rated movies. I have attempted to include only movies without profane or abusive language. Some, however, may carry a few expletives or the subject matter may be unsuitable for children. Note of this has been made behind the film summary whenever possible.

Please keep in mind that our goal is not to offer video substitutes without *anything* objectionable. How could we possibly do that? Hollywood is not known for presenting biblical principles! Our intention is to point out quality movies for your entertainment and edification, films that will not bombard your senses with crudity or a flagrant disrespect for Christian values. Please use judgment when deciding which films are appropriate for your family's viewing.

WHAT ABOUT R-RATED MOVIES?

I have sought the best way to present R-rated movies in this book. They make up nearly half the films produced each year, and many feature poignant issues that should be discussed, making the category difficult to ignore. After six years of reviewing nearly everything that came out, however, my personal belief is that R-rated material is unnecessary. Whatever the subject matter, filmmakers of the past have discovered through creative picture-making how to present the theme without bombarding your senses with desensitizing language and images. For example:

Theme	Movie
Alcohol Abuse	*The Days of Wine and Roses*
	I'll Cry Tomorrow
Crime	*Public Enemy*
	The Asphalt Jungle
	Crimes and Misdemeanors
Drug Abuse	*The Man with the Golden Arm*
Incest	*Something about Amelia*
Apartheid	*Cry, the Beloved Country*

Take it from one who hunts up video suggestions, no subject in today's cinema is completely new. They may have undergone a facelift, but each theme has already been recognized and usually fairly well treated. Most films gaining the R rating do so, not because of the topic of the film, but due to the use of foul language, explicit sex or brutal violence. Motion pictures such as *Goodfellas, Silence of the Lambs, Boyz "N" the Hood*, etc. are indeed well-made films, but my question to you is this: If you think certain films are negatively affecting the society, then why are you supporting them?

Here is how this book can best serve you concerning the R-rated movies. I will give the film title and a brief synopsis. We will *assume* that the rating is for sexual acts, nudity, language, violence or religion bashing. Rather than focus on the content or quality of these films, I will suggest Video Alternatives, which will deal with the same theme or style as the R-rated movie, but without the objectionable material.

Occasionally, I will make comments on a R-rated film if it has received critical acclaim or reached Academy Award status.

THE ADVENTURES OF HUCK FINN (1993). Elijah Wood, Courtney B. Vance. Adventure—PG (3 or 4 mild expletives, some violence). Politically correct version of the Mark Twain classic. For purists, you may find Wood a little too cute for untamable Huck Finn.

   Vid. Alt.: *Huckleberry Finn* (the 1939 version with Mickey Rooney).

ALADDIN (1992). Disney animated tale about a poor boy who discovers a magic lamp. Rated G, it does contain a few scary moments, but it's full of beautiful animation, a stand-out voice performance by Robin Williams, and although the score doesn't top *Beauty and the Beast*, the story is equally enchanting. Some parents may have problems with the magic, sorcery and spells, but it is a fable about good vs. evil, with positive messages concerning love, honor and self-sacrifice.

ALICE (1990). Comedy—PG13 (2 or 3 uses of language, adultery). Mia Farrow dominates the film as a lapsed Catholic discontented with her life and seeking the answers in mysterious Chinese herbs, intellectualism, and an illicit affair. Woody Allen's latest attempt at seeking meaning for life seems to parody his previous works on the subject.

Vid. Alt.: *Black Narcissus* (1947). Deborah Kerr. Beautifully photographed tale of nuns building a hospital in the Himalayas.

ALIVE (1993). Ethan Hawke, Vincent Spano. Action/drama—R. Based on a true story about a 1972 plane crash in the Andes mountains that resulted in cannibalism on the part of the starving survivors. The film receives its R rating not for Hollywood's usual exploitive material, but for the graphic and rather gruesome depiction of an airline crash, with mangled legs, pieces of metal protruding from bodies, etc. Plus, it contains scenes of survivors eating the dead.

Vid. Alt.: *Survival.* Don't get confused, there are several similar titles, but the 1988 video I'm referring to concerns a family who must survive in the wilderness after a plane crash, with little more than their religious faith to sustain them. It stars Robby Sella and Terry Griffin.

ALL I WANT FOR CHRISTMAS (1991). Thora Birch, Jamey Sheridan, Leslie Nielson. Rated G (the kids tell a few whoppers in order to reconcile their parents). Cute but predictable tale of two kids plotting to reunite their divorced parents.

Vid. Alt.: *The Parent Trap.*

AMOS & ANDREW (1992). Samuel L. Jackson, Nicolas Cage, Dabney Coleman. Rated PG-13. Unfunny comedy about a well-to-do black man who moves into an exclusive neighborhood and is mistaken for a thief.

Vid. Alt.: *The Defiant Ones* with Sidney Poitier and Tony Curtis.

AN INNOCENT MAN (1989). Tom Selleck, F. Murray Abraham. Drama—R (violent prison life, obscene language throughout). A man is framed and sent to prison by crooked cops. It's a brutal film to watch, but you sure won't do anything that will cause your incarceration after viewing it. Good performances by Selleck and F. Murray Abraham.

Vid. Alt.: *I am a Fugitive From a Chain Gang* (1932). A powerful enlightenment of the penal system in the 1920s without bombarding you with today's profanity and screen brutality. A poignant and disturbing performance by Paul Muni.

ANOTHER YOU (1991). Gene Wilder, Richard Pryor. Rated R. Lame comedy about mistaken identity.

Vid. Alt: *Inspector General* (1949). Danny Kaye at his best playing dual roles as a showman mistaken for a villainous general.

ASPEN EXTREME (1993). Paul Gross, Peter Berg, Finola Hughes, Teri Polo. Action/Drama—PG13 (about a dozen obscenities; 3 implied sexual situations; drug use, but with a negative portrayal; brief nudity). A handsome Detroit car worker and his buddy set off for a better life as ski instructors in Colorado. The lead becomes king of the mountain while trying to decide between the sweet blonde or the nasty brunette.

For a "buddy film" try these Vid. Alts.: *Donovan's Reef*, or any of the newly released "road" pictures with Hope & Crosby.

THE BABE (1992). John Goodman. Biography of Babe Ruth—PG (although a great baseball hero, the Sultan of Swat was a lewd, crude, profane man, a glutton, a fornicator, and according to this film, an adulterer). A wonderful performance by Goodman as the "man who built Yankee Stadium" serves to remind us that "all glory is fleeting" and only God remains God.

Vid. Alts.: *The Pride of the Yankees, Take Me Out to the Ballgame*, and *The Jackie Robinson Story*.

BATMAN RETURNS (1992). Michael Keaton, Danny DeVito, Michelle Pfeiffer. The nature of the first Batman was dark, mysterious. *Batman*

Returns is more demonic and silly. Nothing makes sense, as if the writer freaked out on LSD before sitting down at the typewriter.

In this outing, Batman faces the Penguin, who has lived in the sewer ever since he was abandoned as a baby. Of course, he's completely mad and seeks revenge. Then there's Catwoman, a meek secretary until her boss throws her out a 12-story window. Then she becomes Helen Reddy with a bullwhip. She also seeks revenge.

Every kid in America is going to want to see this one, but parents beware: Its PG-13 rating is deceptive. It contains much sexual innuendo, some language, and extreme violence, including two women being tossed off the tops of buildings. Technical credits are all superb, but where Batman left you with hope as evil was vanquished, the sequel leaves you with a feeling of despair.

For a **Vid. Alt.** for kids, try *Bugsy Malone*, a spoof on 1930s gangster movies with a pre-teen cast that includes Scott Baio and Jodie Foster (1976—rated G). Some good songs by Paul Williams and all the machine guns shoot custard.

BEAUTY AND THE BEAST (1991). Charming animation for adults as well as children. Rated G—caution, there are several frightening moments that may be a little too intense for very small children.

   Vid. Alt.: *Lady and the Tramp.*

BENNY & JOON (1993). Aidan Quinn, Mary Stuart Masterson, Johnny Depp. Rated PG (one implied sexual situation, 6 or 7 curse words, brief violence). Whimsical story of a brother overprotecting his mentally impaired sister from a strange young man.

   Vid. Alt.: *Modern Times* (1936). An example of Charlie Chaplin at his most creative. Although Johnny Depp does a nice job at Chaplin-esque routines in *Benny and Joon*, there was no one quite like the Little Tramp himself.

THE BIG BANG (1990). Documentary—R (a few expletives, frank sexual conversations). Pseudo-intellectual discussions concerning the creation of the universe.

   Vid. Alt.: *The Creation* (1987). Well-made biblical version of the creation. Hard to find. Check with your local Christian bookstore.

BIG GIRLS DON'T CRY...THEY GET EVEN
(1992). Youth comedy—PG (a few obscenities,
religious ridicule, running away from home as a
solution to minor problems, and thievery). A
neglected 13-year-old runs away. Would have
been more effective if the filmmakers would have
faced serious issues seriously. Instead, we are
given a tepid comedy full of caricatures and a
simplistic ending.

Vid. Alt.: For teens, *The Chalk Garden*, and for
little kids, *Tobie Tyler*.

BILLY BATHGATE (1991). Dustin Hoffman. Crime
drama—R. Fictional account of Dutch Schultz
and his young protege. The folks at Touchstone
(Disney) present nothing new or anything nearly
stylishly told as Coppola's *The Godfather* or
Scorsese's *Goodfellas*.

Vid. Alt.: *Roaring Twenties* with James Cagney
and Humphrey Bogart.

BINGO (1991). Adventures of a dog who can do
anything. Rated PG (occasional profanity, crude
humor). A real bow-wow.

Vid. Alt.: *Love Leads the Way* (1984). True story
of the man who started the Seeing Eye Dog Foundation. Very moving.

BIRD ON A WIRE (1990). Goldie Hawn, Mel
Gibson. Action/Comedy—PG 13 (sexual innuendo, partial nudity, some obscenity and crude humor, violence). Action-packed, but uninspiring as
Mel and Goldie are chased across the country by
members of a drug cartel.

Vid. Alt.: *His Girl Friday* (1940). Cary Grant,
Rosalind Russell and a superb supporting cast. Not
enough can be said about this four-star screwball
comedy. A battle between the sexes where no one
loses. Pass on the remakes.

BLADE RUNNER (1982). Harrison Ford, Sean
Young, Rutger Hauer. Sci/Fi—R. Moody, extremely violent, over-long, futuristic tale of an
enforcer who "retires" replacants—murderous
human-like robots. First released in 1982, *Blade
Runner* has a cult following mainly for its outstanding art direction and special effects, but the
story is weak and the characters unappealing.

Vid. Alt.: *Forbidden Planet* (1956). Intelligent

sci-fi film derived from Shakespeare's *The Tempest*.

BLAME IT ON THE BELLBOY (1991). Dudley Moore. Comedy of errors—PG13 (language, sexual situations, some crude humor, cartoonish violence). Mistaken identity.

Vid. Alts.: *The Court Jester, The Great Dictator, The Inspector General.*

BLAZE (1989). Paul Newman, Lolita Davidovich. Comedy/Drama—R. About the 1950s affair between governor Earl Long and a stripper.

Vid. Alt.: *The Last Hurrah* (1958). Spencer Tracy and a great supporting cast enliven this story of an aged politician seeking re-election in a corrupt system. Or *The Sweet Smell of Success* (1957) with Burt Lancaster and Tony Curtis.

THE BODYGUARD (1992). Kevin Costner, Whitney Houston. Action/Romance—R. VIP bodyguard is hired to protect a singer/actress from an obsessed fan. The film seems to be a loving tribute to Steve McQueen. Costner dons a hair style reminiscent of McQueen's. So too is every move and piercing glance given by our hero. Costner does a nice job as always, but just as he is no Errol Flynn, so too he is no Steve McQueen.

Vid. Alt. *Bullitt* (caution, does contain a few expletives and some violence, but nothing like today's lack of standards).

BONFIRE OF THE VANITIES (1990). Tom Hanks, Melanie Griffith, Bruce Willis. Satire—R. Unfaithful screen rendition of the Tom Wolfe bestseller about a Wall Street wizard's world slowly crumbling apart after his mistress runs down a black man.

Vid. Alt.: *Executive Suite* (1954). Corporate corruption. Excellent cast—William Holden, Fredric March, Barbara Stanwyck, Shelley Winters.

BOOMERANG (1992). Eddy Murphy. Comedy—R. An ad exec who uses women has the tables turned on him. A very crude movie. The film should be insulting to black women, black men, and everybody else.

17

Vid. Alt.: *Mr. Lucky* (1943). Cary Grant as a sharp con man who goes straight with the help of Laraine Day.

BORN YESTERDAY (1993). Don Johnson, Melanie Griffith, John Goodman. Comedy—PG (several profanities from Goodman character ruined what might have been a pleasant film-going experience).

Vid. Alt.: The original *Born Yesterday* with Judy Holliday or *The Hucksters* with Ava Gardner.

BOYZ 'N THE HOOD (1991). Larry Fishburne, Ice Cube, Cuba Gooding, Jr. Drama—R. Gripping tale of three boys growing up in a south-central L.A. neighborhood.

Vid. Alt.: *The Cross & the Switchblade* (1972). Pat Boone, Erik Estrada. True story of Dave Wilkerson, working with street gangs.

BRAIN DONORS (1992). John Turturro. Slapstick comedy—PG (lots of sexual innuendo, one scene with Playboy pinups). A Marx Brothers imitation from the creators of *Airplane*.

Vid. Alt.: *Animal Crackers.*

BRENDA STARR (1992). Brooke Shields. Adventure/spoof—PG (one scene with implied sex, a dozen or so obscenities from one character). Brenda's on the trail of a story about a fuel-saving potion, hoping to scoop the competition and save her paper, *The Flash*. Shields is perfect as the cartoon ace reporter come to life, but the script lacks wit and soon becomes tedious.

Vid. Alt.: *His Girl Friday* (1940). Rosalind Russell proves to be an ace reporter in this battle of the sexes, screwball comedy. Also stars Cary Grant.

A BRIEF HISTORY OF TIME (1992). Documentary PG. Presents the origins of the universe according to Stephen Hawking, the brilliant physicist who's confined to a wheelchair by ALS. He gives several theories—many of which conflict—as to how we came about.

Vid. Alt.: *The Creation* (1987). Well-made biblical version of the Creation. Ask for it in Christian bookstores.

BUFFY, THE VAMPIRE SLAYER (1992). Kristy Swanson, Luke Perry, Paul Reubens. Comedy/horror—PG13 (about a dozen expletives, one profanity, reincarnation, some violence—but it's comic-book like, one suggestive sexual remark). A valley girl vs. vampires in Beverly Hills. For sure!

For a **Vid. Alt.** spoofing horror movies: *Abbott & Costello Meet Frankenstein*—and Dracula, and the Wolfman...very, very funny.

BUGSY (1991). Warren Beatty, Annette Bening. Drama—R. Bio of gangster Bugsy Siegel, whose dream was to turn a small desert town called Las Vegas into a gambling empire.

Vid. Alts.: *The Killing, Little Caesar, Kiss of Death,* and *White Heat.*

CAPE FEAR (1992). Robert DeNiro, Nick Nolte, Jessica Lange. Thriller—R. Darker, more violent version of the 1962 film with Robert Mitchum and Gregory Peck. An ex-con terrorizes the family of a lawyer he blames for his incarceration. Great acting, with another strong performance by newcomer Juliette Lewis *(Crooked Hearts)*. Martin Scorsese keeps his record intact by directing another picture focusing on the darker side of mankind. This film brutalizes not only the characters in the story, but the viewers as well.

Vid. Alt.: The '62 classic *Cape Fear.* As good as DeNiro is, Mitchum's psychopathic portrayal is just as convincing without subjecting us to brutal beatings and bloodletting.

CHAPLIN (1992). Robert Downey, Jr., Geraldine Chaplin, Kevin Dunn, Dan Ackroyd, Moira Kelly. Biography—PG13 (about a dozen profanities and obscenities, a very brief scene with nudity, implied sexual situations, dim view of FBI tactics). Bravura performance by Downey as the first comic film genius. Tastefully made and very funny moments from actual Chaplin movies.

Vid. Alt.: *Chaplin—A Character is Born; Charlie Chaplin: The Funniest Man in the World.*

CHRISTOPHER COLUMBUS, THE DISCOVERY (1992). George Corraface, Tom Selleck, Rachel Ward, Marlon Brando. Adventure—PG13 (some violence, lots of native nudity). Unusual casting, sluggish direction, faulty representation of history.

Vid. Alt.: *Mutiny on the Bounty* (the 1935 version).

CITY OF JOY (1992). Patrick Swayze. Drama—PG13 (profanity and obscene language from our hero, violence and extreme brutality, graphic birth scene in a leper village, suggested promiscuity). A discontented doctor seeks peace by moving to Calcutta. Gee, I know that's where I'd go!

Vid. Alt.: Documentary on Mother Teresa (hard to find, but worth the effort, as it is a life-changing film).

CITY SLICKERS (1991). Billy Crystal. Comedy—PG13 (several profanities and obscenities). Three yuppies want to make a change in their lives, so they go on a cattle drive. Very funny, moving story with strong messages dealing with loyalty, comradeship, and self-examination. When the Billy Crystal character is asked, "Would you cheat on your wife if nobody would ever know?" he answers with, "I'd know." Now, that's character. We don't see a lot of that in today's cinema. Except for a few unnecessary words, this is a terrific comedy.

CLASS ACTION (1991). Gene Hackman, Mary Elizabeth Mastrantonio. Drama—R. Father and daughter face off on opposite sides of a class-action suit.

Vid. Alt.: *Adam's Rib* (1949). A literate battle-of-the-sexes script with Spencer Tracy facing off against Katharine Hepburn in an attempted murder trial.

CLIFFHANGER (1993). Sylvester Stallone. Action—R. A rescue team encounters a murderous madman and his team of hijackers on top of the Rocky Mountains (doubled by the Italian Alps Dolemite Range). The same non-stop action found in the Indiana Jones pictures, but the script (co-written by Stallone) contains insipid, inane, pretentious and profane dialogue throughout. Uncalled for murderous violence including the shocking deaths of the film's two comic reliefs. Long on action, short on scenario.

Vid. Alt.: *Indiana Jones & The Last Crusade.* Caution: contains some violence and one profanity for which the culprit is immediately punished). Funny, thrilling. Sean Connery and Harrison Ford are terrific.

COME SEE THE PARADISE (1990). Dennis Quaid, Tamlyn Tomita. Drama—R. A romance set during WWII's internment of Japanese-Americans, with the film-makers' often one-sided view of history.

Vid. Alt.: *The Bridge on the River Kwai* (1957). Won several Oscars including Best Picture. About POWs forced to build a bridge for the Japanese. A must-see.

COP & A HALF (1993). Burt Reynolds, Norman D. Golden II. Action/Comedy—PG (3 or 4 expletives, violence). An 8-year-old partners up with a police detective after he witnesses a murder.

Vid. Alt.: A true bonding of man and child, *Captain Courageous* (1937), with Spencer Tracy and Freddie Bartholomew.

COURAGE MOUNTAIN (1989). Juliette Caton, Charlie Sheen. Romance/adventure—PG (the scenes of war are graphic, too intense for little ones, but there is no language or nudity). The continuing story of Heidi. Except for the few war scenes, this is one for the whole family.

Vid. Alt.: *Heidi* (1937). There are several remakes of this classic Johanna Spyri tale. Shirley Temple did it in 1937. None of the films lives up to the book. By all means have your kids read it. There's a great deal of Christian symbolism that didn't make it into the film versions.

CRY BABY (1990). Johnny Depp. Musical comedy—PG13 (sexual references, language, Christianity ridiculed).

Vid. Alt.: *Babes on Broadway* (1941). Considered by many as the best of the Rooney/Garland musicals.

THE CRYING GAME (1992). Stephen Rea, Miranda Richardson, Forest Whitaker. Romantic thriller—R. A simple story about an English soldier kidnapped by members of the IRA develops into a complex romantic thriller.

Vid. Alt.: *The Manchurian Candidate* (1962). Outstanding performances by Frank Sinatra, Laurence Harvey and Angela Landsbury. Political thriller about a brainwashed man set to assassinate the President incumbent. Video also contains an interview with Sinatra and the film's director, John Frankenheimer.

CURLY SUE (1991). James Belushi, Kelly Lynch. Comedy—PG (another "family" film with a dozen or so uncalled-for profanities). Lady lawyer takes in a homeless con artist and his little girl. Like the society we live in, Hollywood doesn't want to seriously face the subject of the homeless, so the audience is subjected to this drivel.

Vid. Alt.: *A Little Princess*, Parts 1, 2, 3. Made-for-TV version stars Maureen Lipman, Amelia Shankley. Young Sarah comes to live at a boarding school in Victorian London. However, upon her father's death and the loss of his fortune, she finds a bitter change in store. This Dickens-like tale relates well to children without boring the adults. Teaches compassion, but caution is suggested. Some may object to the Hindu statues of gods and goddesses and the reference to magic as life's benefactor rather than God. But it presents examples of cruelty and compassion with an uplifting finale.

THE CUTTING EDGE (1992). D. B. Sweeney, Moira Kelly. Romantic comedy—PG (a dozen or so obscenities and profanities, suggested promiscuity). A film by the numbers, no surprises, and yet a feel-good film about an ice skater and an ex-hockey player who team up for the Olympics.

Vid. Alt.: *Pat & Mike*.

DANCES WITH WOLVES (1990). Kevin Costner. Western—PG13 (a few profanities and obscenities, some crude humor that's despised by the hero, rear male nudity, intense violence, one scene of sex out of wedlock). A disillusioned Union officer makes peace with himself and the Sioux in South Dakota. An epic film full of humor and pathos.

Vid. Alt.: *Cheyenne Autumn* (1964). John Ford epic about the mistreatment of the Indian.

DAVE (1993). Kevin Kline, Sigourney Weaver, Ben Kingsley. Comedy—PG13 (a few expletives, 2 or 3 profanities, one sexual situation, no nudity). A charming Capra-esque film about a look-a-like who poses for a stroke-stricken President. I deplore the uncalled-for profanity, but the film is uplifting, funny and full of poignancy.

Vid. Alt.: *Mr. Smith Goes to Washington* (1939). Jimmy Stewart as an idealist who finds himself fighting for the ordinary guy in the Senate. A very moving and perceptive Frank Capra film and one of the best-made films of all time.

DAYS OF THUNDER (1990). Tom Cruise, Robert Duvall. Action—PG13 (several uses of obscenity and profanity, two sexual situations). The hottest movie star in the world set in the competitive world of NASCAR racing.

Vid. Alt.: *Bullitt* (1968). Steve McQueen and the greatest car chase ever filmed. (Caution: Some language and violence, but nothing compared to today's standards—or lack of standards.)

DEADLY CURRENTS (1992). A powerful, insightful documentary look at the Palestinian-Israeli conflict. Winner of several prestigious awards, the film has a *60 Minutes* feel to it, yet when expanded to the silver screen, you get a much more horrifying look at an ongoing cycle of violence on the streets of the West Bank and Gaza. The film also indicts the media, showing that television is a kind of filter and revealing how some members of the media actually cause incidents. Not yet rated, it certainly is not for children. There are a few obscenities spoken and, of course, war-torn violence; explicit shots of wounded victims, including children. Filmmaker Simcha Jacobovici gives a balanced look at this most tragic and frustrating battle between Arabs and Jews. An important film.

DIAMOND'S EDGE (1988). PG (for mild violence). Boring English detective spoof.

Vid. Alt.: *Murder By Death* (1976). All-star cast in a Neil Simon spoof of the detective genre.

DIGGSTOWN (1992). James Woods, Lou Gossett, Jr., Bruce Dern. Action/drama—R. Hustler Woods cons town owner Dern into betting against 48-year-old fighter Gossett, who must battle 10 boxers—in one day! If you give four stars to *The Sting* for its adroit script and colorful performances, then *Diggstown* would only garner one.

Vid. Alt.: *Requiem for a Heavyweight.*

THE DISTINGUISHED GENTLEMAN (1992). Eddie Murphy. Comedy—R. A con artist discovers being a member of Congress can be the biggest scam of all.

Vid. Alt.: *Mr. Smith Goes to Washington.*

DOC HOLLYWOOD (1992). Michael J. Fox, Barnard Hughes, Julie Warner. Comedy—PG-13 (several obscenities, brief nudity). Painfully silly story about a Beverly Hills-bound plastic surgeon detoured into a small country town.

For nonsense done well, try this **Vid. Alt.:** *What's Up, Doc?* (1972). Barbra Streisand and Ryan O'Neal in a slapstick classic.

THE DOCTOR (1991). William Hurt, Christine Lahti, Elizabeth Perkins. PG-13 (3 or 4 obscenities, some lewd and dark humor). A non-feeling doctor learns compassion from other patients after discovering he has cancer.

Vid. Alt.: *The Last Angry Man* (1959). Paul Muni in a sentimental story of a simple doctor whose life is going to be presented on TV. Muni, the forgotten star, is outstanding in this and almost every other picture he made.

DRACULA (1992). Gary Oldman, Winona Ryder. Horror—R. In the '30s and '40s horror films such as *Dracula, Frankenstein* or *The Cat People* were actually morality plays where good was triumphant over evil. In the '70s and '80s they became little more than a showcase for the studio special effects department. Good vs. evil was replaced with the sinister Freddie Kruger or Jason returning sequel after sequel trying to kill as many randied teenagers as possible in 96 minutes.

Now we have Francis Ford Coppola entering the genre with his version of Dracula. But this time the Count is an omnipresent creature who contemptuously burns a crucifix with a stare, rather than turning away from the significance of the cross—something the vampire has done ever since Bela Lugosi first put on a set of fangs. This new twist changes the entire theme of the Dracula legend. No longer does God conquer the devil; now man does.

Vid. Alt.: *Cat People* (the 1942 version—pass on the inferior and obscene 1982 version).

DRIVING MISS DAISY (1989). Jessica Tandy, Morgan Freeman, Dan Aykroyd. PG (one profanity). Very entertaining, gentle film about a cantankerous old Southern woman and the new chauffeur she would just as soon do without. Deals well with serious subjects such as civil rights and old age.

ENCINO MAN (1992). Sean Astin, Brendan Fraser. Teen comedy—PG (4 or 5 obscenities from the bad guy, lots of leering at girls in tight dresses, but moralistic lessons about not using people). Two high schoolers find a Cro Magnon man frozen in the backyard. They thaw the stone-ager out, hoping he will make them popular. If you are able to turn off your intellect, you may find some laughs; otherwise, this comedy will be best accepted by pre-teens and cavemen.

ENEMIES, A LOVE STORY (1989). Ron Silver, Anjelica Huston. Drama—R. A Holocaust survivor finds himself married to three women.

    Vid. Alts. about victims of the Holocaust: *The Diary of Anne Frank* (1959), *The Hiding Place* (1975), *Hanna's War* (1988), *The Wanness Conference* (1984).

ETHAN FROME (1993). Liam Neeson, Joan Allen, Patricia Arquette. Period drama—PG (depressing themes of unhappy marriage and adultery). Classic tale of unhappily married man who falls in love with a younger woman.

    Vid. Alts.: *Love with the Proper Stranger* (Caution: contains adult themes), or *Great Expectations*.

FAR AND AWAY (1992). Tom Cruise, Nicole Kidman. Epic adventure drama—PG13 (paints a picture of the bigotry toward the Irish in America 100 years ago; the couple lives in a bordello but no sex or nudity is shown; about a dozen profanities and a lot of pugilistic violence). A poor farmer and a spoiled rich girl escape Ireland during the late 1800s for a better life in America. Once there, they soon discover the harsh realities awaiting the Irish.

    Vid. Alt.: The fortieth anniversary edition of *The Quiet Man*, the 1952 John Ford classic with John Wayne and Maureen O'Hara. There are a few similarities between the two films, but where *Far and Away* is both earthy and violent, *The Quiet Man* is a gentle, warm, romantic comedy full of blarney.

A FAR OFF PLACE (1993). Disney adventure—PG (two obscenities, violence including murder, native mystical teachings).

    Vid. Alt.: *Cheetah* (1989). Disney adventure with two kids and a young Masai raise an orphaned cheetah.

FERN GULLY (1992). Voices of Robin Williams, Christian Slater, Tim Curry and Samantha Mathis. Animation—G (a few scary moments as the evil force materializes; also, nature is governed by enchanted spirits, humanism is preached). Story centers on an imaginary Rain Forest governed by fairies. Hexxus (an evil, destructive force long since entrapped by the fairies) escapes, using man to destroy all the trees. Unfortunately, the ecology message misses the mark. I'm afraid it's man who's to blame for the destruction of the environment, not the evil Hexxus. I could not find a video suitable for children dealing with this subject, but there is a book available at the library entitled *50 Simple Things Kids Can Do To Save The Earth*, published by The Earthworks Group. It explains the ozone hole, water and air pollution, spending energy wisely, etc. Parents, you might want to pick it up and see if you find it suitable for your children.

A FEW GOOD MEN (1992). Tom Cruise, Jack Nicholson, Demi Moore. Military courtroom drama—R. When a marine is killed by the actions of two fellow non-coms, a hot-shot military lawyer discovers the defendants were ordered to harass the victim.

Vid. Alt.: *The Caine Mutiny.*

FINAL ANALYSIS (1992). Richard Gere, Kim Basinger. Erotic thriller—R. Another Hitchcock wannabe. It has some nice moments, but a bit too convoluted to be taken seriously.

Vid. Alt.: *Vertigo.*

FIRE IN THE SKY (1993). D. B. Sweeney, Robert Patrick, James Garner. Based on a so-called true story about a man who was abducted by aliens. Rated PG-13 (some language, violence, frightening scenes as aliens probe a human aboard a spaceship). Poorly made, poorly acted.

Vid. Alt.: *The Day the Earth Stood Still* (1951). A sci-fi drama about an alien coming to earth to warn humans of eminent destruction from nuclear bombs. 4-star acting, script and musical score.

THE FISHER KING (1992). Jeff Bridges, Robin Williams. Com/Dra—R. After the world of a top-rated radio shock-jock falls apart, he learns compassion from those who live on the street. Some important messages are discussed, and strong performances by all. Still, the film goes on and on and never quite reaches its goal.

Vid. Alt.: *They Might Be Giants* (1971). George C. Scott giving the best impersonation of Sherlock Holmes since Basil Rathbone. Joanne Woodward as a psychiatrist (named Watson) trying to treat a psychotic, but winds up involved in his adventure. Some very funny moments. (Caution: Contains a few profanities.)

FOLKS (1992). Tom Selleck and Don Amechi. Comedy—PG13 (profanity and obscenity, violence, attempted suicide as a means to solve life's problems, two sexual situations between a married couple, and brief backside nudity). Not wanting to be a burden in their old age, an elderly couple convince their son to help do them in. How's this for bad taste—in one scene the son pours gasoline over his parents as they sit in their car! What in the world was Selleck thinking when he took this project?

Vid. Alt.: *Dad*—rated PG for 1 profanity, 2 expletives, but contains a positive message about the importance of working at family relationships. Ted Danson and Jack Lemmon star in this moving and uplifting comedy.

FOREVER YOUNG Mel Gibson, Jamie Lee Curtis, Elijah Wood. Fantasy—PG (a few expletives used to point out the difference between acceptable language in 1939 and the present, brief nude shot of Gibson, one fight scene between Gibson and a man trying to rape Curtis). A WWII test pilot volunteers for a cryogenics experiment; 50 years later he is defrosted and has to adjust to a new life.

Vid. Alt.: *The Amazing Mr. Blunden* (G-rated film for children). *Enchanted Cottage* (1945) with Robert Young and Dorothy McGuire. Lovely fantasy about a scarred war vet and a homely woman, both made beautiful by their love. Very romantic film.

1492: CONQUEST OF PARADISE (1993). Gerard DePardieu. Adventure—PG13 (one profanity, brief native nudity—but not exploitative, signs of the brutality of the Spanish Inquisition, with strangulations and burnings at the stake, representatives of the Catholic church portrayed as anything but loving men of God, graphic battle scenes, and once again, a movie shows someone vomiting.) Badly told story of Christopher Columbus.

27

Vid. Alt.: *Mutiny on the Bounty* (the 1935 version).

FREDDIE AS F.R.0.7. Rated PG (contains a couple of sexual references and some unflattering stereotypes, including African-Americans represented as streetwise black crows; a couple of scenes may be frightening for very young children). Animated tale of a prince who's turned into a frog and banished to the forest pond. Soon he grows to the size of a man and becomes a secret agent for the French government. The premise is silly, the animation kin to Saturday morning cartoon quality, the songs uninspiring, and the humor negligible.

Vid. Alt.: *The World of Hans Christian Anderson.*

GHOST (1990). Patrick Swayze, Demi Moore, Whoopi Goldberg. Romantic adventure—PG13 (some language and profanity, violence, murder, promiscuity, revenge and a bizarre concept of the spirit world). After being murdered, a ghost warns his girlfriend (through a psychic) that the killer is now after her. Interesting story, but spiritually way off the mark.

Vid. Alt.: *The Ghost and Mrs. Muir* (a gothic romance without promiscuity).

GLENGARRY GLEN ROSS (1992). Al Pacino, Jack Lemmon, Ed Harris, Alan Arkin, Alec Baldwin. Comedy/Drama—R. Based on the award-winning play, the screenplay is made up largely of profane and obscene language, with the F-word being used over 100 times. Other critics love it. The question you should ask yourself: "Is great acting reason enough to attend a movie?"

Vid. Alt.: *Death of a Salesman* (the 1951 outstanding version with Fredric March is not yet on video; Dustin Hoffman's 1985 TV presentation is available on both video and laser disk).

THE GODS MUST BE CRAZY II (1989). Comedy—PG (several expletives). Once again, a South African villager discovers the "civilized" Western world has gone out of control.

Vid. Alt.: *Shooting Africa* (1988), documentary about wildlife on the Dark Continent.

GOODFELLAS (1991). Robert DeNiro, Ray Liotta, Joe Pesci. Gangster drama—R. Martin Scorsese has made a brilliant film in the category of *The*

Godfather, but it is extremely negative to the spirit, not to mention the Italian/American community. Contains sadistic violence and an overwhelming use of profanity and obscenity.

Vid. Alt.: *The Killing* (1956). Sterling Hayden, Elisha Cook, Jr., Jay C. Flippen. A gritty telling of a heist that goes wrong. Its laconic, documentary-like narration may date it a bit, but still a sharp-edged Stanley Kubrick classic.

GRAND CANYON (1992). Danny Glover, Kevin Kline, Mary McDonnell. Comedy/drama. A "forties-something" look at the age we live in. What at first seems pop-psychology soon turns out to be rather insightful. The homeless, crime and violence in our society, despair, loneliness—calamities that touch each of us are presented without sermon, and often with perceptive humor.

Each character looking for an answer comes close to discovering the world's true salvation when they are awed by the majesty of the Grand Canyon. What they may not be grasping, however, is that the true miracle and solace lie not in the grandeur of the creation, but in the One who created it. Unfortunately, this quality film is justly rated R for obscene language throughout, some violence, surgical procedures and brief nudity.

GREEN CARD (1990). Gerard Depardieu, Andie MacDowell. PG 13 (2 obscenities, deceit). Romantic comedy (without promiscuity) about a marriage of convenience so a Frenchman can stay in the U.S. A warm comedy, if you can overlook the attempt to pull a fast one on the Department of Immigration.

Vid. Alt.: *Barefoot in the Park* (1967). Robert Redford, Jane Fonda. A very good adaptation of Neil Simon's very funny play about newlyweds.

THE GRIFTERS (1990). John Cusack, Anjelica Huston. Rated R. Mother and son con artists.

Vid. Alt.: *The Asphalt Jungle* (1950). Set a standard for crime dramas. An aged criminal plans one last heist. Adroit performances by Sam Jaffe and Marilyn Monroe in a small part.

GROSS ANATOMY (1989). Matthew Modine, Daphne Zuniga, Christine Lahti. PG13 (language, sexual situations, anatomical dissections). The trials and tribulations of first-year medical students. Nice acting, but *Gross Anatomy* is a fitting title.

Vid. Alt.: *The Hospital* (1971). Caution: Although this has a 4-star script by Paddy Chayefsky and performance by George C. Scott, the material is often irreverent and profane. It's unmatched in its satirical look at the medical profession, but beware the language and adult subject matter.

GUILTY AS SIN (1993). Rebecca DeMornay, Don Johnson. Thriller—R. Handsome Don is a gigolo accused of murdering his rich wife. Beautiful Rebecca is the hot-shot lawyer defending him. Good performances and suspenseful script.

Vid. Alt.: *Anatomy of a Murder*.

THE GUN IN BETTY LOU'S HANDBAG (1992). Penelope Ann Miller. Comedy—PG13 (a few obscenities sprinkled throughout, two shockingly violent scenes of murder). A put-upon librarian falsely confesses to a murder to gain attention from her neglecting husband. Funny and bright performances from Alfre Woodard and Cathy Moriarty, but the story is senseless.

Vid. Alt.: *The Man Who Knew Too Much*.

HAPPILY EVER AFTER (1993). Animated—G. Described as a sequel to *Snow White and the Seven Dwarfs*, yet falls short of the quality and charm of the Disney classic.

Vid. Alt.: *Snow White and the Seven Dwarfs*.

HEART CONDITION (1990). Bob Hoskins, Denzel Washington. Action/comedy—R. After a heart attack, a bigoted cop gets a heart transplant from a black lawyer he hated.

Vid. Alts. dealing with race relations: *All God's Children* (1980). Richard Widmark and Ossie Davis in a story about forced busing. An excellent made-for-TV movie. *The Autobiography of Miss Jane Pittman* (1974), memories of a 110-year-old black woman who was born into slavery. *The Defiant Ones* (1958). Two escaped convicts, one black (Sidney Poitier), one white (Tony Curtis). Screenplay won an Oscar.

HERO (1992). Dustin Hoffman, Andy Garcia, Geena Davis. Comedy—PG13 (crude, obscene and profane language throughout). A low-life con artist grudgingly rescues survivors of a downed aircraft, only to have another down-and-outer steal the glory and the million-dollar reward. To "update" the Frank Capra/Good Neighbor Sam genre, this film presents *all* of its characters as cynical and unlikable, and furnishes them with the same 4-letter word vocabulary once associated with drunken sailors. Frank Capra didn't do that, and not just because of the restrictions of the times. He was a storyteller, and a storyteller uses the language—he doesn't abuse it.

Vid. Alt.: *Meet John Doe*, or if you can catch *American Madness* late some night, by all means VCR it!

HOFFA (1992). Jack Nicholson, Danny DeVito. Bio—R. DeVito directed this extenuating portrait of a teamster who was little more than a gangster.

Vid. Alt.: *The Last Hurrah, On the Waterfront, Never Steal Anything Small, Brother John.*

HOME ALONE (1990). Macaulay Culkin. Comedy-PG (cartoonish violence). An 8-year-old boy is accidentally left home alone and has to defend his house against two inept burglars.

HOME ALONE 2 (1992). Macaulay Culkin, Joe Pesci, Daniel Stern. Comedy—PG (the cartoon-like violence of its predecessor is taken to extremes, with bricks being tossed at people from rooftops and nail guns firing into the nose of one character). Our pre-teen hero gets lost in the big city, only to confront the same nemeses from his last adventure. If you object to your children watching Tom & Jerry because of the violence, then you'll probably want to pass on this film as it is as close to being a Wile E. Coyote cartoon as any live-action movie can get.

Vid. Alt.: *Road Runner vs. Wile E. Coyote: The Classic Chase.*

HONEYMOON IN VEGAS (1992). Nicolas Cage, James Caan, Sarah Jessica Parker. Comedy—PG13 (fornication, profanity, obscenity, gambling, sexual situations). A marriage-shy NY detective loses his girlfriend in a poker game.

A sometimes funny screwball comedy, but for a superb **Vid. Alt.**, try *A New Leaf* with Walter Matthau and Elaine May (caution: a few obscene words, but nothing compared to today's lack of standards).

HOOK (1992). Robin Williams, Dustin Hoffman. Fantasy—PG (two expletives, comic-book action). Peter Pan has grown up and has forgotten who he once was—until Captain Hook extracts revenge. Kids will love it. Teaches a good lesson about the family unit.

HOUSESITTER (1992). Steve Martin, Goldie Hawn. Comedy—deceptively rated PG (promiscuity, several obscenities and profanities, a few crude sexual jokes, constant lying). A pathological liar moves into a man's house, without his knowledge, and sets up home, telling members of the community she is his new bride. It's kind of *Fatal Attraction* set to comedy.

Vid. Alt.: *What's Up Doc?* (does contain some lying, but the culprits are punished for it. And it's a whole lot funnier).

HOWARD'S END (1992). Anthony Hopkins, Emma Thompson. Period drama—PG (adult subject matter, but contains no obscenity, nudity or excessive violence). A placid and thoughtful look at the mores of the English aristocracy circa 1920s. A Masterpiece Theatre-type production rich with passion, conflict and something rare in today's cinema...taste.

THE HUNT FOR RED OCTOBER (1990). Sean Connery. Rated PG (5 or 6 profanities, 1 scene with violence). Cold war thriller about a Russian defecting with a nuclear sub—or is he? Except for the profanities, which I abhor, it is an excellent film.

Vid. Alt.: *Run Silent, Run Deep* (1958). Clark Gable and Burt Lancaster vs. the Japanese. Three-star submarine action.

IMMEDIATE FAMILY (1989). Glenn Close, James Woods, Mary Stuart Masterson. Comedy—PG13 (several uses of profanity and obscenity). Unable to have children of their own, a successful middle-aged couple decide to adopt. The film shows the responsibility and sanity of giving birth. Only the language seemed to be offensive.

Vid. Alt.: *Yours, Mine & Ours* (1968). Lucille Ball, Henry Fonda and 18 kids! Funny and often touching.

INDECENT PROPOSAL (1993). Robert Redford, Demi Moore, Woody Harrelson. Drama - R. Years ago Albert Brooks asked in *Broadcast News*, "Do you know what the devil looks like?...He looks like Robert Redford." In *Indecent Proposal*, Redford proves the statement true. A dramatic version of *Honeymoon in Vegas*, with a wealthy eccentric offering to pay a million dollars to spend one romantic night with another man's wife.

For a romantic **Vid. Alt.:** *Love Affair* with Irene Dunne and Charles Boyer.

INDIAN RUNNER (1991). Rated R. Gritty modern-day Cain & Able story by first-time director Sean Penn. Strong performances, with an ingratiating supporting role by Charles Bronson. Well-told story, with unsatisfying ending both theologically and thematically.

Vid. Alt.: *East of Eden* (1954 version). Classic Cain and Abel theme. James Dean in his first starring role.

INDIAN SUMMER (1993). Diane Lane, Vincent Spano, Elizabeth Perkins, Bill Pazton, Alan Arkin. Comedy - PG13 (peppered with profanity and obscenity, pot smoking, another film where several attractive leads are smokers, several crude sexual remarks, one sexual situation, implied sexual relations outside marriage, brief nudity). A group of thirty-somethings are invited back to the summer camp of their youth. In the style of *The Big Chill*, with the same angst-ridden middle-agers looking for answers. Often funny, but very transparent, and don't look for any spiritual awakenings here, because none of these people do.

Vid. Alt.: *The Rules of the Game*. (Hard to find, but this film shows the folly and decadence of mankind. Keep in mind, one can learn from the mistakes of others.)

INTERNAL AFFAIRS (1990). Richard Gere, Andy Garcia. Action/thriller—R. A very intense movie about Internal Affairs tracking a bad cop.

Vid. Alt.: *Detective Story* (1951). Good cast headed by Kirk Douglas as a police detective struggling with the evils of society. Adult subject matter, tastefully handled.

JACK THE BEAR Danny DeVito. Comedy/drama - PG13 (several profanities, some violence, and the abduction of a small child). Depressing tale of widower and his two sons coping with the loss of the mother while living next door to a psychopathic version of Boo Radley.

Vid. Alt.: *To Kill a Mockingbird.*

JACOB'S LADDER (1990). Tim Robbins. Horror—R. Confusing and directionless plot about a man who may or may not be dead.

Vid. Alt.: *Cat People* (1942 version starring Simone Simon, Kent Smith—don't make the mistake of renting the 1982 remake; besides being an inferior film, it also contains extreme violence, nudity and language.) I do not recommend horror films, but like many old classic spook stories, the original *Cat People* is a morality play. In one scene our hero holds up a cross and tells the menacing foe to "leave us alone in the name of God." Slowly, the possessed leopard retreats. You won't find that kind of symbolism in today's slasher movies.

JESUS OF MONTREAL (1989). Lothaire Bluteau. Rated R (perversion of Bible Scriptures, profanity, sexual situations, blasphemy). The star of the Passion Play of Christ becomes overwhelmed with the part. Like with *The Last Temptation of Christ*, this film also corrupts the Scriptures.

Vid. Alt.: *Jesus of Nazareth* (1977).

THE JETSONS: The Movie (1990). Animated with rock & roll music. Rated G - a letdown for Jetsons fans.

Vid. Alt.: *Animal Farm* (1955). Animated classic of George Orwell's political satire. Fun for kids and adults.

JFK (1991). Kevin Costner. Rated R. *"JFK* is an act of execrable history and contemptible citizenship by a man of technical skill and negligible conscience." George F. Will, syndicated columnist *L.A. Times*, 12/24/91.

I am less than an authority concerning the assassination of President Kennedy. Like many Americans, I believe there is more to the story than the public knows. I am, however, cautious when it comes to Oliver Stone's interpretation of history. Both conservatives and liberals are fast to acknowledge Stone's "dramatic license" with historical facts. Politics aside, Oliver Stone is very

perceptive concerning the power and suggestive-
ness of the film medium and he's in top form here
with a film that will cause you to think and discuss.
Just remember that Stone's conception of politics
is kindred to Martin Scorcese's religious views
(The Last Temptation of Christ). Viewer beware!

Vid. Alt.: *The Manchurian Candidate.*

JURASSIC PARK (1993). Richard Attenborough,
Laura Dern, Sam Neill. Action/Adventure - PG13
(2 or 3 curse words; the non-stop frightening action
is much too intense for small children, with the
heroes being chased by extremely real-looking
dinosaurs). There are no Video Alternatives for
this film. It has to be experienced to be believed.
Truly no expense has been spared.

KNIGHT MOVES (1992). Christopher Lambert,
Diane Lane, Tom Skerritt. Suspense/thriller - R.
A chess player is suspected of killing single wom-
en.

Vid. Alt.: *Wait Until Dark.* Caution: This is a
scary movie but it won't bombard your senses with
today's visual and verbal obscenities. It is a well-
crafted thriller about a blind woman being terror-
ized by a murderer. Stars Audrey Hepburn.

K2 Michael Biehn, Matt Craven. Adventure - R (some
profanity, obscenity and, of course, a few people
falling off the tallest mountain in the world).
Traditional film about men bonding as they attempt to conquer nature.

Vid. Alt.: *Survival* (1988). Not a great film, but
positive message about a family surviving in the
wilderness with the help of their Christian faith.
With Robby Sella and Terry Griffin.

LADYBUGS (1992). Rodney Dangerfield. PG13
(language, cross-dressing, crude humor, incluing
sophomoric jokes about teenage sex, homosexual-
ity, and pedophilia). Rodney recruits a boy to play
on a girl's soccer team.

Vid. Alt.: *The Parent Trap, The Red Balloon, A
Boy Named Charlie Brown, The Best of the Little
Rascals.*

THE LAST OF THE MOHICANS (1992). Daniel
Day-Lewis, Madeline Stowe. Action/Adventure -
(battle brutality, including nearly 100 killings,
many with gruesome scalpings).

Vid. Alt.: *Drums Along the Mohawk* (1939). A deft script set amid the Revolutionary War. Complete with action, romance and humor. Directed by John Ford, featuring his stock acting troupe, including Henry Fonda, Ward Bond, and John Carradine. Or, for a musical comedy dealing with this time period, try *1776*, about the men who wrote our Declaration of Independence.

LATE FOR DINNER (1991). Brian Winmer, Peter Berg. Comedy about two men waking up 29 yeas after being frozen by a cryonics researcher. PG (profanity and obscenities throughout). Great premise but the writer fails to bring life to his script.

Vid. Alt.: *Metropolitan* (1989).

A LEAGUE OF THEIR OWN (1992). Tom Hanks, Geena Davis, Madonna. Comedy - PG (vulgar humr and language associated with baseball dugouts). Funny film about the forming of a woman's baseball league in the '40s.

Vid. Alt.: *Take Me Out to the Ballgame* (1949). Turn-of-the-century musical with Frank Sinatra and Gene Kelly.

LEAP OF FAITH (1992). Steve Martin, Debra Winger, Liam Neeson. Drama/Comedy - PG-13 (seeral profanities, obscenities, blasphemy, an implied sexual situation, cynicism). A con artist posing as a faith healer/evangelist. It does expose some fraudulent practices, but its cynical premise assumes all traveling preachers are out to take us.

Vid. Alt.: *Cotton Patch Gospel* (hard to find, but worth the effort; try local Christian book stores).

LEAVING NORMAL (1992). Christine Lahti, Meg Tilly. Comedy/drama - R. Whiny tale of twowomen, battered by men and life, traveling together to Alaska in search of happiness.

Vid. Alt.: *Ship of Fools* (caution: some adult subject matter).

LIFE WITH MIKEY (1993). Michael J. Fox, Christina Vidal. Comedy - PG (2 or 3 uncalledfor obscenities toward the beginning, stealing, and the lead character smokes—although the statement is made about how bad cigarettes and secondary smoke can be). A has-been child actor now operates a kids' talent agency. The discovery of an

11-year-old latch-key delinquent may be the answer to the agent's unsuccessful business.

Vid. Alt.: *Sorrowful Jones* or the 1934 version of *Little Miss Marker*.

LISTEN UP: THE LIVES OF QUINCY JONES (1990). Documentary - PG13 (several uses of profanity and obscenity).

Vid. Alt.: *Young Man With a Horn* (1950). Loosely based on the life of jazz great Bix Beiderbecke.

THE LITTLE MERMAID Walt Disney animation - G (some sorcery is suggested). As in all Disney films, there is an all-powerful witch, but, as in all Disney films, Evil is defeated by the powers of Good. It is a well-made picture, destined to stand among other classics such as *Sleeping Beauty* and *Snow White*. The music is great, especially the rousing "Under the Sea."

LORENZO'S OIL Susan Sarandon, Nick Nolte. Drama - PG13 (a sick boy deteriorates, a couple of profanities, adult subject matter including implied sexual situations and the helplessness one feels for sick children). Based on a true story of parents trying to find a cure for their sick child. Uplifting, yet very difficult to view.

Vid. Alt.: *Joni.*

LOST IN YONKERS (1993). Richard Dreyfuss, Mercedes Ruehl, Irene Worth. Neil Simon comedy - PG (4 or 5 profanities). Funny, often touching story of two boys having to go live with their cantankerous grandmother and their simple-minded aunt. Hindered only by the use of Christ's name as if it were a mere expletive. The message needs to be sent to the "Land of Make-Believe" that profanity is extremely offensive to many of us.

Vid. Alt.: *Auntie Mame.*

MADDOG & GLORY (1993). Robert DeNiro, Bill Murray, Uma Thurman. Action/comedy - R. A mild-mannered police photographer saves the life of a mobster and, in return, finds a girl at his door as payment.

Vid. Alt.: *After the Fox* - 1966 comedy with Peter Sellers as a con man posing as a film director.

MADE IN AMERICA (1993). Whoopi Goldberg, Ted Danson. Comedy - PG13 (some crude sexual humor, one sexual situation, and lots of profanity and obscenity). An African-American teenager discovers her mother had been artificially inseminated and to the surprise of everyone, the father is not only white, but a used-car salesman!

Vid. Alt.: *Teacher's Pet.*

MADHOUSE (1990). John Larroquette, Kirstie Alley. Comedy - PG13 (language, violence, lewdness, vulgarities). A happy couple is invaded by crude houseguests.

Vid. Alt.: *Mr. Hobbs Takes a Vacation* (1963). James Stewart has to spend summer vacation with his kids, their spouses and the obnoxious grandchildren. Very funny.

THE MAN IN THE MOON (1991). Lovely coming-of-age film about two teenage sisters in love with the same boy. Unfortunately, it contains language and sexual situations (PG-13).

Coming-of-age Vid. Alt.: *I Know Why The Caged Bird Sings* (1979). Diahann Carroll, Ruby Dee. Trenchant script of black youth growing up in 1930s rural south. *Nicholas Nickleby* (1946 version with Cedric Hardwicke). Dickens' story about a poor family and their wealthy, but villainous uncle. Great adventure. Also a well-made 1987 animated version for kids. *A Tree Grows in Brooklyn* (1945). Peggy Ann Garner, Dorothy McGuire. Turn-of-the-century coming-of-age film. Won several awards.

MAN TROUBLE (1992). Jack Nicholson, Ellen Barkin, Beverly DiAngelo. PG13 (sexual references/situations, profanity and obscenity sprinkled throughout, and brief violence). An unscrupulous owner of a down-and-out attack dog service falls for a client. Could be called a comic/thriller/romance, but it doesn't work in any of those categories. Still, Nicholson, as always, is fun to watch with that sly, cynical edge he gives to every line.

Vid. Alt.: *Father Goose* or *The Bachelor and the Bobby Soxer*, both starring Cary Grant and both excellent examples of the struggle between men and women.

MEDICINE MAN (1992). Sean Connery, Lorraine Bracco. Romantic adventure - PG13 (obscene and profane language throughout, native nudity). Well-intentioned but cliched tale of scientist trying to discover the cure for cancer in South America, only to be threatened by the destruction of the Rain Forest.

Romantic **Vid. Alt.:** *The Wind and the Lion*

MEMOIRS OF AN INVISIBLE MAN (1992). Chevy Chase, Daryl Hannah. Comedy/action - PG13 (profanity and obscenity sprinkled throughout, two sexual situations, promiscuity). A rogue CIA agent attempts to catch a man who's been accidentally made invisible. Chevy's attempt to showcase a darker side of himself consists of a constant use of profanity.

Vid. Alt.: *The Invisible Man* (1933). Don't be put off by the age of this film It's a 4-star morality play that holds up. Claude Rains gives a great voice performance in this classic story by H. G. Wells.

MEMPHIS BELLE. Matthew Modine, Eric Stoltz, John Lithgow. PG-13 (small amount of ribald language considering the setting; implied illicit sex, intense battle scenes). True story of first B-17 crew to complete 25 missions over Germany. Exquisite period details enhance this tale of ten "ordinary" heroes.

Vid. Alt.: *Hell is for Heroes.*

MERMAIDS (1990). Cher, Winona Ryder. Comedy/Drama - PG13 (several profanities and obscenities, and two sexual situations). Eccentric single mother raising two daughters.

Vid. Alt.: *You Can't Take It With You* (1938). All-star cast in very funny Frank Capra film about a very eccentric family. Won Best Picture. The remake is okay, but not up to the original.

METROPOLITAN (1990). Featuring an unknown but very talented cast. Comedy/Drama - PG13 (3 or 4 obscenities). Story of the new lost generation, caught up in coming-out parties and fruitless conversations about politics, sex, and social mores. A very literate, funny picture showing the shallowness of life without a spiritual development.

Vid. Alt.: *The Sun Also Rises* (the 1957 version).

THE MIGHTY DUCKS (1992). Emilio Estevez. Kid's Comedy - PG (a dozen or so mild expletives, boys looking at a men's magazine, after which one boy says, "It's nothing I haven't seen on MTV," mild hockey rink fighting, one scene depicting drinking and driving for which the culprit is punished, a couple of crude sexual innuendos). Forced to do community service, a hot-shot lawyer serves as coach to a losing kids hockey team. *The Bad News Bears* without the wit.

Vid. Alt.: *Tom Thumb* or *Home Alone* (caution: *Home Alone* contains slapstick violence and one scene where a child is reading an adult magazine, but the film does contain positive messages).

MISERY (1990). James Caan, Kathy Bates. Thriller/suspense - R (some brutality toward the end, three expletives). She's his biggest fan, so she keeps him prisoner in her home.

Vid. Alt.: *Wait until Dark* (1967). Scary drama about a blind woman (Audrey Hepburn) being menaced by a murderer (Alan Arkin).

MOM AND DAD SAVE THE WORLD (1992). Teri Garr, Jeffrey Jones (the maniacal principal from *Ferris Bueller's Day Off*), Jon Lovitz. Comedy - PG (a couple of off-color jokes, scantily clad women, and one scene in which cute giant mushrooms suddenly sprout little sharp teeth and menace the hero). A nonsensical comedy about the ruler of a small distant plant, obsessed with blowing up Earth. Kids may enjoy it, but it will be laborious for adults to sit through.

Vid. Alt.: *The Brave Little Toaster*. A creative, animated story that presents positive messages about friendship, loyalty and self-sacrifice.

MO' MONEY. Damon Wayans, Marlon Wayans, Stacy Dash. Comedy - R. To impress a girl he just met, an out-of-work hustler gets a job at her credit card company. He steals a card so he can take the girl to fancy nightclubs. Soon he gets caught by his boss, who's also stealing from the company. Our hero is then blackmailed into stealing big time. After a while he tells his boss he wants out. That's when the shooting starts. The message here: Scamming's okay, so long as you don't take too much and don't get caught.

Vid. Alt.: *It's a Mad, Mad, Mad, Mad World*. No one gets away with a thing, but you'll laugh your head off watching them try.

MOUNTAINS OF THE MOON (1990). Patrick Bergin. Adventure - R. Friendship and betrayal intertwine in this account of 19th-century explorers Richard Burton and John Hanning Spede's perilous expedition to discover the source of the Nile.

Vid. Alt.: *Stanley and Livingston* (1939). A bit dated, but uplifting story of journalist looking for the famous humanitarian in darkest Africa.

THE MUPPET CHRISTMAS CAROL (1992). Michael Caine and the Jim Henson creations. The Great Gonzo and Rizzo the Rat serve as tour guides through this Charles Dickens classic about the redemption of Ebenezer Scrooge. As for the scary moments in this G-rated musical, the gang at Disney and Jim Henson Productions delicately handle these scenes, presenting humor to ease children out of any fright they may experience. Paul Williams' musical numbers are life-affirming with such positive lyrics as "Life is Full of Surprises, Every Day is a Gift." As for you parents, be grateful for Michael Caine. He balances humor and pathos perhaps better than any present-day movie star and he makes us believe not only in his character, but in the puppet antics as well.

Vid. Alt.: (for kids) *Mr. Magoo's Christmas Carol*; (for adults) *The Gathering*.

MUSIC BOX (1989). Jessica Lange. Drama - PG13 (one or two uses of profanity, descriptions of gruesome acts). An attorney must defend her father, who is accused of wartime atrocities.

Vid. Alt.: *Judgment at Nuremberg* (1961). Trial of Nazi war crimes. All-star cast includes Spencer Tracy, Burt Lancaster, Marlene Dietrich and Maximilian Schell. A four-star film, winner of several awards.

MY COUSIN VINNY (1992). Joe Pesci. Rated R. New York novice attorney defends his cousin of bogus murder in Alabama. Funny performances, but beware the brutal language.

Vid. Alt.: *The Prisoner of Zenda* (1937 Ronald Colman version—pass on the remakes).

MY GIRL (1991). Anna Chumsky, Macaulay Culkin. Comedy/drama - PG (a few obscenities, death of a loved one). One summer in the life of two 11-year-old best friends. Caution: The death of one child will need to be discussed with your kids.

Vid. Alt.: *To Kill a Mockingbird.*

NARROW MARGIN (1990). Gene Hackman, Ann Archer. Suspense - R. Bad guys out to get the eyewitness of a murder.

Vid. Alt: *Double Indemnity* (1944). Film noir/ suspense with an outstanding supporting performance by Edward G. Robinson.

NATIONAL LAMPOON'S CHRISTMAS VACATION (1989). Chevy Chase. PG13. Christmas at the Griswalds' is like a Jerry Lewis movie updated to the '80s, by including needless obscene language, profanity and lots of crude humor.

Slapstick Vid. Alt.: *Monkey Business* with the Marx Brothers. *The Party* with Peter Sellers. *The Disorderly Orderly* with Jerry Lewis.

NEWSIES (1992). Christian Bale, Robert Duvall. Musical - PG (cigarette smoking, mild violence). Disney version of the 1899 NYC newspaper boys' strike against tycoons Joseph Pulitzer and William R. Hearst.

Vid. Alt.: *Oliver* - 1968 musical version of the Dickens classic *Oliver Twist.*

THE NIGHT WE NEVER MET (1993). Matthew Broderick, Annabella Sciorra, Kevin Anderson. Romantic comedy - R. Three people, looking for a getaway place, co-op an apartment through a broker. Never meeting, each resides in the rented room two days a week. Romance ensues only to be hindered by mistaken identity.

Vid. Alts. about mistaken identity: *Along Came Jones, As You Like It, Charley's Aunt.*

NOISES OFF (1992). Michael Caine, Carol Burnett, Julie Hagerty, John Ritter. Screwball comedy/ farce - PG13 (lots of profanity, especially from Ritter, sexual entendres, Nicollette Sheridan spends most of the film running around in her underwear). A high-speed, hilarious play within a play about an acting ensemble preparing for Broadway. Unfortunately, superfluous profanity prevents my recommendation.

Vid. Alt.: *Stage Door* (1937). All-star cast includes Ginger Rogers, Katharine Hepburn, and

Lucille Ball as young women trying to make it in show business.

OF MICE AND MEN (1992). Gary Sinise, John Malkovich. Drama - PG13 (profanity sprinkled throughout). Well-made version of the Steinbeck classic with screenplay by Horton Foote (*Tender Mercies, To Kill a Mocking Bird, A Trip to Bountiful*).

   Vid. Alt.: *Of Mice and Men* (the 1939 version with Lon Chaney, Jr., and Burgess Meredith).

ONCE UPON A CRIME (1992). Richard Lewis, Cybill Shepherd, Sean Young, John Candy, James Belushi. Screwball comedy - PG (a dozen obscenities, some sexual innuendo inappropriate for children). Siskel & Ebert called *Stop! Or My Mom Will Shoot* the worst movie of the year. They obviously haven't seen this epic. Can film-goers really become accustomed to mediocrity? They can if instead of the talents of a Danny Kaye or the Marx brothers they're given Richard Lewis and Jim Belushi. Name me one good film Jim Belushi has been in!

   Vid. Alt.: *The Bank Dick, What's Up, Doc?, It's a Mad, Mad, Mad, Mad World, The Party, A Shot in the Dark, The Time of Their Lives.*

OTHER PEOPLE'S MONEY (1991). Danny De Vito, Gregory Peck. Comedy satire - R. A high roller tries a company takeover.

   Vid. Alt.: *The Battle of the Sexes* (1960). Peter Sellers. From a James Thurber short story, a sophisticated comedy about a hostile business takeover.

PACIFIC HEIGHTS. Melanie Griffith, Michael Keaton. Thriller - R. A psycho moves in with a young unmarried couple.

   Vid. Alt.: *Gaslight, Cape Fear* (1962 version) or *The Two Mrs. Carrolls.*

PARADISE (1991). Don Johnson, Melanie Griffith, Elijah Wood, Thora Birch. PG-13 (brief nudity, fornication, a few expletives). A moving narrative of a young boy moving in with a man and wife who recently lost their own child. Very good performances by all. My main objection is the male lead's disdain for church-going and Christians in general.

43

Vid. Alt.: *The Parent Trap* (1961). Hayley Mills. A warm family comedy about twins trying to reconcile their divorced parents.

PATRIOT GAMES (1992). Harrison Ford, Anne Archer, Richard Harris. Action/drama - R. An ex-CIA agent foils an attempted abduction of members of the Royal family. He spends the rest of the film eluding vengeful members of the IRA.

A well-made film, but for foreign intrigue without the R-rated material, try this **Vid. Alt.:** *The Third Man* (1949). Orson Welles, Joseph Cotton. A film noir about cold war intrigue.

THE PLAYER (1992). Tim Robbins, Greta Scacchi, and cameos by many stars. Comedy/drama - R. A behind-the-scenes look at Hollywood deal-making, while a studio exec murders a writer.

Vid. Alt.: *Sunset Blvd.* (1950). Gloria Swanson stars as Norma Desmond, an aging silent film star desperately seeking a comeback. Or, *The Bad and the Beautiful* (1952). Kirk Douglas and Lana Turner head an all-star case about an ambitious producer who will use anyone to get what he wants.

POINT OF NO RETURN (1993). Bridget Fonda. Action - R. Inferior remake of the French film *La Femme Nikita*, about a convict recruited by a CIA-type organization to be a hit-woman.

Vid. Alt.: *Gun Crazy* (caution: I am referring to the 1949 version, not the 1992 remake).

THE POWER OF ONE (1992). Stephen Dorff, Morgan Freeman. Drama - PG13 (violence, boxing, bigotry). Well-meaning, if sometimes over-stated story of apartheid and its effect on a white boy growing up in Africa.

A far superior **Vid. Alt.:** *Cry, The Beloved Country*, a 4-star 1951 film about a black minister trying to make a difference in South Africa.

PRELUDE TO A KISS (1992). Alec Baldwin, Meg Ryan. Comic fantasy - PG13 (5 or 6 profanities, implied sex before marriage, a kiss between two men). An eccentric young couple meet, fall in love and quickly marry. At the reception, a strange old man kisses the bride. Because he wishes he could be young again and she wishes to have his confidence, a soul transference occurs. She is now in his body, he in hers. Nice performances by all, but the metaphysical theme is no better handled here than in *Ghost* or *Freaky Friday*.

Vid. Alt.: *Beauty and the Beast*, the 1946 French version. It's hard to find and it does contain subtitles, but it's worth it. A 4-star masterpiece.

PRESUMED INNOCENT (1990). Harrison Ford. Suspense - R. A well-written "thinker's" movie I'd like to be able to recommend; however, like most serious films of this era, it has several offenses, including nudity, adultery, and profanity.

Vid. Alt.: *The Wrong Man* (1956). True story of a man wrongly accused of robbery. Stars Henry Fonda and Vera Miles, and directed by Alfred Hitchcock.

PRETTY WOMAN (1990). Richard Gere, Julia Roberts. Comedy - R. Rich Richard turns street girl Julia into a lady, learning some life lessons himself along the way. The screen morality of the '80s/'90s prevents my recommending this very touching comedy. It never reaches Shaw's *Pygmalion*. Rather, it remains in Hollywood's all too comfortable territory, becoming only "My Fair Streetwalker."

Vid. Alt.: *My Fair Lady* (1964). Rex Harrison, Audrey Hepburn. Four-star musical based on Pygmalion. *Pygmalion* (1938). A good adaptation of George Bernard Shaw's play, but it may move a bit slowly for today's audiences. Still, there is some very good dialogue. Leslie Howard, Wendy Hiller.

PROBLEM CHILD. John Ritter. Comedy - PG (some crude humor, some bad language). A couple adopts a little boy only to discover he's a real brat.

Vid. Alt.: *Laurel and Hardy: Brats.* Stan and Ollie play dual parts as they babysit their kids.

Q & A (1990). Nick Nolte, Timothy Hutton. Action/Drama - R. One good cop trying to nail one very bad cop. Directed by adept moviemaker Sidney Lumet, the film portrays a very corrupt society.

Vid. Alt.: *Detective Story* (1951). Kirk Douglas as a hard-boiled cop with a secret.

QUIGLEY DOWN UNDER (1990). Tom Selleck. Western - PG13 (violence, several obscenities). A western, Australian style.

Vid. Alt.: *Shane* (1953). A remarkable Western starring Alan Ladd.

RADIO FLYER (1992). Drama - PG13 (language—both profanity and obscenity sprinkled throughout, child abuse, fantasy about being able to fly). A disturbing film, it tries to appeal to kids on a fantasy level, but it also presents a serious look at child abuse. One or the other would have been great subjects, but together, the film will disappoint and perhaps frighten little ones.

A **Vid. Alt.** that adults will enjoy with the little ones: *The Red Balloon* (1956). Enchanting children's fable about a boy who befriends a magical balloon that follows him everywhere.

RAMBLING ROSE. Robert Duvall, Laura Dern, Diane Ladd, Lukas Haas. Drama/comedy about a young southern girl looking for love. A great score, beautiful cinematography, and sensitive performances by all. Unfortunately, it's justly rated R for two sexual situations and the usual dosage of unnecessary profanity and obscenity. I found this film less offensive than most recent PG films due to its honest handling of family ideals and its prevailing moralistic attitudes. But be warned, most will be offended by a sexual situation between Dern and Haas.

Vid. Alt.: *To Kill a Mockingbird* (1962). Four-star, gentle classic about a southern lawyer defending a black man accused of rape in the 1930s South. Brilliant film that shouldn't be missed. Stars Gregory Peck and, in his first film role, Robert Duvall as Boo Radley. (Caution, one scene could be frightening for small children.) *Tender Mercies* (1983). Robert Duvall (caution, a few obscenities from our hero until a widow has an effect on his life.) A country singer on the skids is helped to get his life together by a religious widow.

THE RAPTURE. Mimi Rogers. R (explicit sexual scenes with nudity and perversity, profanity, two shocking acts of violence). A discontented woman becomes a Christian during the last days.

This is a subject that has not been dealt with very often, but for a **Vid. Alt.**, contact your Christian bookstores for Mark IV Videos, which presents a top rental series in the Christian marketplace on the tribulation and last times. The series begins with *A Thief in the Night, A Distant Thunder, Image of the Beast* and *Prodigal Planet*. This is not this reviewer's favorite series. I found these films to be extremely outdated, but there are some very effective statements about the future and, as I say, they remain top rentals. People are very concerned with the role of the Christian in the last times. These films attempt to take a serious look at this provocative subject.

RESCUERS DOWN UNDER. Disney animated sequel to *The Rescuers*. Rated G (some frightening scenes for younger children).

> **Vid. Alt.:** *Animal Farm* (1955). Great political satire for adults, amusing animation for children.

REVENGE. Kevin Costner, Anthony Quinn, Madeleine Stowe. Drama/action - R. A self-serving American falls in love with the wife of his friend, a ruthless Mexican power broker.

> **Vid. Alt.:** *M* (1931). Dated, but frightening revenge tale concerning a child molester brought to justice by vigilantes. German with subtitles. Stars Peter Lorre.

RICH IN LOVE (1992). Albert Finney, Jill Clayburgh, Kathryn Erbe, Suzy Amis. Drama about a Southern family coping with the matriarch's abandonment. Rated PG-13 (sexual situations, alcohol abuse, 2-3 profanities, adult themes including the discussion of abortion). Boring letdown by the director of *Driving Miss Daisy*.

> **Vid. Alt.:** *Driving Miss Daisy*.

A RIVER RUNS THROUGH IT (1992). Craig Sheffer, Brad Pitt, Tom Skerritt, Emily Lloyd. Drama - PG (several profanities and obscenities, alcohol abuse, one fight scene). Robert Redford directs this heartwarming tale of two brothers growing up in Montana during the 1920s. Based on the book by Norman MaClean, the story is very Hemingway-esque, putting emphasis on character rather than action. Redford went to great efforts to preserve the language of the book and takes care in presenting the family's pastime and earth connection—fly fishing. One of the best films of the year, but due to the language I cannot recommend it.

May I suggest the **Vid. Alt.** *To Kill a Mockingbird* or *Trip to Bountiful.*

THE ROCKETEER (1991). Bill Campbell, Jennifer Connelly, Alan Arkin, Paul Sorvino, Timothy Dalton. Action/adventure - PG (4 or 5 expletives and comic-book action). A rocketpack attached to any hearty young daredevil's back will cause him to fly. It's 1938 and, of course, the Nazis want such a device. Enter the Rocketeer, who must defend the American way of life by preventing the Germans from gaining possession of the rocket. Lots of fun.

ROCKY V (1990). Sylvester Stallone. Drama - PG13 (boxing ring violence, a few expletives from the "bad guys"). In the same day, Rocky is informed that another boxing bout could be fatal *and* a business manager has absconded with all his money. What to do? Manage a young fighter, what else? John G. Avildsen's soporific direction and Stallone's predictable screenplay prove to be the KO factors for this series.

Vid. Alt.: *Rocky* (1976). Forget the sequels, but the original was quite powerful. Won Best Picture that year.

ROGER & ME (1989). Serio/comic documentary about the decision of Roger Smith, GM's chairman, to close plants in Flint, Michigan, causing over 30,000 people to lose their jobs. Well received by film critics. Rated PG (four or five obscenities, two off-color jokes).

THE SANDLOT (1993). Kid's comedy - PG (a few mild expletives, one graphic scene where the kids get sick after chewing tobacco). The new boy in town struggles to become a member of the neighborhood baseball team. So far this year, the best of the kid films. A pleasure to view.

Vid. Alt.: *The Little Rascals.*

SHATTERED (1991). Tom Berenger, Bob Hoskins. Mystery/suspense - R. Poorly written, badly directed story of an amnesiac trying to discover his past. Extremely loud sound effects and ridiculous script make this an example of "how not to make a movie."

Vid. Alt.: *Spellbound* (1945). Ingrid Bergman, Gregory Peck. A psychiatrist helps an amnesiac accused of murder. Hitchcock classic!

SHINING THROUGH (1992). Michael Douglas, Melanie Griffith. Romantic/action - R. A '40s-style spy thriller set in WW2, diminished with today's profane language and superfluous sexual situations.

Vid. Alt.: *Casablanca, Charade, Foreign Correspondent.*

SHOW OF FORCE (1990). Amy Irving, Lou Diamond Phillips. Rated R. A reporter is drawn into an important story about official corruption in Puerto Rico.

Vid. Alt.: *Touch of Evil* (1958). Charlton Heston, Orson Welles (caution: adult subjects). About corruption in a small border town.

SIDEKICKS (1993). Jonathan Brandis, Chuck Norris, Joe Piscopo, Mako, Beau Bridges. PG (chopsocky violence, a couple of expletives). Same story line as *Karate Kid*, with undernourished nerd winning the Grandmaster Tournament and defeating the local bully with the help of Asian mentor. This version has the added ingredient of Chuck Norris as our young hero's idol. Positive messages, including working hard and believing in yourself to make your dreams come true.

SILENCE OF THE LAMBS (1991). Jodie Foster, Anthony Hopkins. Thriller - R (hard core gore and murder, sexual situations — including transsexualism, brutal language). Suspenseful psychological thriller about the FBI using a jailed psychopath to catch a serial killer. **Lasting negative images.**

Vid. Alt.: *Cape Fear* (1962 version).

SISTER ACT (1992). Whoopi Goldberg. Comedy - PG (a few obscenities sprinkled throughout and an off-screen murder). A lounge singer hides out in a convent after witnessing her gangster boyfriend murder one of his underlings. The film is very predictable, but it comes alive when Whoopi, dressed as a nun, takes charge of the church choir. Except for the few bad words, it is a feel-good movie.

SKI PATROL (1990). Ray Walston, Martin Mull. Comedy - PG (sexual innuendo, some language, crude humor—what little there is—one use of profanity). Some great ski footage, but even the kids will be bored with this lame comedy about an evil land developer trying to steal a ski resort.

Vid. Alt.: Hope and Crosby's road pictures: *To Bali*, *To Rio*, *To Hong Kong*, *To Utopia*.

SPLITTING HEIRS (1993). Eric Idle, Rick Moranis, John Cleese, Catherine Zeta, Barbara Hershey. Comedy - PG13 (crude sexual innuendo, including near incest, language including profanity, attempt at murder, sexual situations, mocking of authority figures). A young man discovers he was switched at birth. How to regain his rightful place as Duke of Bournemouth? For some inexplicable reason, try murder.

Vid. Alt.: *Kind Hearts and Coronets* (caution, contains theme of murder to gain an inheritance). Alec Guinness playing multiple roles in a very funny English comedy about a man setting out to inherit the family title by first eliminating his other relatives.

STAR TREK VI (1991). William Shatner and the crew of the Enterprise attempt to rescue their worst enemies from extinction. Rated PG (some violence, two obscenities and a subtle reference that the creation is merely myth). A "politically correct" space opera smothered in Shakespeare and served with irony. Marginally better than *Star Trek V* due to sure-handed direction.

Vid. Alt.: *Forbidden Planet* (1956). Walter Pidgeon, Leslie Nielson, Anne Francis. Intelligent sci-fi film about space explorers landing on a planet ruled by one man and an evil force. Plot derived from Shakespeare's *The Tempest*.

STEEL MAGNOLIAS (1989). Sally Field, Shirley MacLaine, Dolly Parton, Daryl Hannah. Comedy/Drama - PG (some off-color humor, brief rear male nudity in a locker-room scene, profanity). Story of six strong-minded Southern belles coping with life. Definitely some sincere performances, but I was offended by the portrayal of men. It seems the only way Hollywood knows how to make a strong woman's picture is to make the men weak and insensitive.

Vid. Alt.: *The Women* (1939). Dated, but still amusing tale of high society from a feminine viewpoint. All star/all female cast.

STELLA (1990). Bette Midler, John Goodman. Drama - PG13 (some profanity, crude humor and sexual situations). Heavy-handed direction ruined this tale of a woman who sacrifices everything for her daughter.

Vid. Alt.: *Stella Dallas* (1937 version). Tearjerker, but a work of art compared to the 1989 remake.

A STRANGER AMONG US (1992). Melanie Griffith. Police/drama - PG13 (some violence, two or three crude sexual comments, a few profanities and obscenities. A hardened NY police detective trying to solve a murder in the Hasidic community. Not much of a suspense who committed the crime, but a respectful look at the ultra-Orthodox Jewish sect.

Vid. Alt.: *Detective Story*, a taut police action without the objectionable language, starring Kirk Douglas.

STRICTLY BALLROOM (1993). Farcical comedy - PG (about a dozen obscenities). A very original, dark-humored film about a couple attempting to win a dance contest on their own terms.

Vid. Alt.: *The Gay Divorcee* with Fred and Ginger.

SWING KIDS (1992). Robert Sean Leonard, Christian Bale, and a superb unbilled performance by Kenneth Branagh. Rated PG-13 (2-3 profanities, violence). 1930s Germany.

Vid. Alt.: *The Diary of Anne Frank.*

TEENAGE MUTANT NINJA TURTLES (1990). Fantasy/Action Comedy - PG (a few expletives, violence). The comic book characters are now "lean, mean and on the screen," fighting for the rights of hapless citizens. Also contained in the story are the New Age teachings of telepathy and visualization, which may be offensive to some viewers.

Vid. Alt.: *Bugsy Malone* (1976). Musical spoof with kids as gangsters. Their guns shoot whipped cream. Scott Baio, Jodie Foster.

TEENAGE MUTANT NINJA TURTLES II (1993). Action adventure aimed at kids. PG (kick-box violence). The producers send the turtles back in time. Unfortunately, not far enough.

Vid. Alt.: *The Little Rascals.*

TEXASVILLE (1990). Jeff Bridges, Cybill Shepherd. Comedy/Drama - R. Lackluster sequel to *The Last Picture Show*; includes Christian-bashing.

Vid. Alts. about small-town life: *Our Town, The Trip to Bountiful, The Human Comedy*.

THELONIUS MONK: STRAIGHT NO CHASER (1988). Documentary of one of the primary architects of modern jazz with a rare look at his idiosyncratic approach to playing the piano and leading a band. Rated PG13 (two or three obscene words). Although this is far from my favorite type of music, I found it fascinating to watch a true artist at work. Produced by jazz buff Clint Eastwood.

THIS IS MY LIFE (1992). Julie Kavner, Gaby Hoffman, Samantha Mathis. Comedy - PG13 (frank sexual dialogue, one sex scene, 2 or 3 obscenities, no profanity). Story of single standup comedian and the effect her budding career has on her two neglected daughters. The scenes between the girls and their mom are effective, but the comedy routines are more like something you'd see on the Fox Network—forced and often amateurish. Really inane and somewhat annoying musical score from the normally gifted Carly Simon.

For great stand-up comedy routines on video: *Bill Cosby, Himself* (caution: 2 or 3 expletives) or *Billy Crystal: Midnight Train to Moscow* (caution: one vulgar statement toward the beginning of the video; other than that, a very "clean" and funny concert with several poignant vignettes and stand-up routines by Billy as the first U.S. comedian to appear in Moscow).

THREE MEN AND A LITTLE LADY (1990). Tom Selleck, Ted Danson. Comedy - PG (4-5 expletives and a little girl's innocent inquiry about the male anatomy). Corny but very funny sequel. Robin Weisman will steal your heart as the little girl.

Vid. Alt.: *Father's Little Dividend*.

THUNDERHEART (1992). Val Kilmer, Sam Shepard, Graham Greene. Action/drama - R. The FBI investigates a murder on the Indian reservation.

Vid. Alt.: *The FBI Story* (1959). James Stewart

stars in this episodic tribute to J. Edgar Hoover and the Bureau.

TOTAL RECALL (1990). Arnold Schwarzenegger. Sci/Fi Action - R. Special effects are superior, the story itself exciting, but the violence becomes overwhelming and desensitizing.

> **Vid. Alt.:** *Forbidden Planet* (1956). Walter Pidgeon, Leslie Nielsen, Anne Francis. Intelligent sci-fi film about space explorers landing on a planet ruled by one man and an evil force. Plot derived from Shakespeare's *The Tempest*.

TOYS (1992). Robin Williams. Fantasy - PG-13 (several expletives, crude sexual humor, one sexual situation, 2 profanities, violence, including a father trying to kill his own son, anti-military themes). A joyless movie about the son of a toymaker trying to prevent his retired military uncle from making war toys at the factory. Inappropriate for kids, boring for adults. One of the worst films of the year. The set designs are elaborate, but as Roger Ebert accurately assessed, "It's a movie all dressed up, but with no place to go."

> **Vid. Alt.:** *Babes in Toyland* (the 1934 version with Laurel and Hardy; great to watch with the kids).

29TH STREET (1991). Danny Aiello. Comedy/drama - R. True story of the volatile family life of the first New York State Lottery winner.

> **Vid Alts.** about family life: *A Family Upside Down, The Gathering, Islands in the Stream* (caution, contains a few obscenities).

THE TWO JAKES (1990). Jack Nicholson. Drama - R. Atmospheric sequel directed by Nicholson, hampered by out-of-place profanity.

> **Vid. Alt.:** *The Maltese Falcon* (1941). The quintessential detective film with Humphrey Bogart. Four stars. They don't get any better than this!

UNFORGIVEN (1992). Clint Eastwood, Morgan Freeman, Gene Hackman. An aging gun fighter is brought out of retirement to hunt down two men who brutally scarred a woman's face. Rated R (one sexual scene, profane and crude language throughout, violence). The production shows the power of the medium, by aligning the audience with murderers. And unlike westerns of the past, *Unforgiven*'s good guys behave almost as poorly as the villains.

Hackman gives a superb performance, but for a western **Vid. Alt.** with social comment, but lacking crudity or screen brutality, try *The Ox-Bow Incident* (1943), with Henry Fonda. A lynch mob takes the law into its own hands. A 4-star script, with outstanding performances.

UNTAMED HEART (1992). Christian Slater, Marisa Tomei. Rated PG-13 (sexuality and sexual situations, no nudity, violence including a brutal attempted rape, some drinking, several profanities and obscenities). Melodramatic love story complete with a life-threatening illness.

Vid. Alt.: *Brian's Song* (1970). True story of best friends Brian Piccolo and Gale Sayers (the Chicago Bears) dealing with Piccolo's cancer. A 4-star TV movie.

USED PEOPLE (1992). Shirley MacLaine, Marcello Mastroianni, Jessica Tandy, Kathy Bates. Romantic comedy - PG13 (just a few expletives, one obscenity for which the culprit is reprimanded; several characters are mentally unstable, including a little boy who thinks he has super-human abilities, putting his life in jeopardy on several occasions). A charming movie about a middle-aged woman and her eccentric family adjusting to the death of her husband and a suitor who wants to marry her.

Vid. Alt.: *A Brivele Der Mamen* (A Letter to Mother), 1938 film in Yiddish with subtitles. A moving story about a Jewish mother's efforts to hold her family together.

VITAL SIGNS (1990). Jimmy Smits, Diane Lane. Rated R. Did you ever want to know what third-year medical residents go through? Most critics panned this film.

Vid. Alt.: *The Last Angry Man* (1959). Paul Muni in his last film, as a beloved doctor.

WAITING FOR THE LIGHT (1990). Shirley MacLaine, Teri Garr. Comedy - PG (four expletives, implied adultery, borderline mockery of religious beliefs). Story of eccentric family who pull a practical joke on a hermit, only to have the incident pronounced a miracle by the community.

Contains a few laughs but disappointing considering the cast.

WAR OF THE ROSES (1989). Michael Douglas, Kathleen Turner, Danny DeVito (also directing). Rated R. Dark comedy about a hostile divorce. This film will disturb you. DeVito takes a poisonous look at the times we live in and gives marriage a black eye.

  Vid. Alt.: *The Lion In Winter* (1968). Peter O'Toole, Katharine Hepburn. Fabulous costume drama about Henry II and his wife, Eleanor of Aguitane. Won several awards including Hepburn's third Oscar. (Caution, adult subject matter.) Some of the best movie dialogue ever!

THE WATERDANCE (1992). Eric Stoltz, Wesley Snipes, William Forsythe, Helen Hunt. Drama - R (frank sexual talk, adultery, brief nudity, alcohol abuse, obscene language throughout). Story of several men coming to terms with being wheelchair-bound for life.

  Vid. Alt.: *Joni* (1980). True story of a girl who must rebuild her life after a debilitating accident.

WAYNE'S WORLD (1992). Dana Carvey. PG13 (a few profanities, lots of sexual innuendo, several tall girls in short skirts). The long version of a Saturday Night Live skit. Funny and very, very stupid. No way will there be a sequel! Way!!

  Vid. Alt.: *Animal Crackers*.

WE'RE NO ANGELS (1989). Robert DeNiro, Sean Penn. Comedy/Drama - R. As in *Family Business*, criminals are portrayed as heros.

  Vid. Alt.: *We're No Angels* (1955 version).

WHERE THE HEART IS (1990). Stars Dabney Coleman, directed by John Boorman and produced by mistake! Comedy about a father trying to get his spoiled grown children to support themselves. Rated R.

  Vid. Alt.: *Mr. Hobbs Takes a Vacation* (1962). Jimmy Stewart tries to spend summer vacation with his offspring. Often hilarious.

WHITE SANDS (1992). Willem Dafoe, Mickey Rourke, Mary Elizabeth Mastrantonio, and cameo by Mimi Rogers. Action - R. A convoluted suspense thriller about a good cop trying to nab crooked FBI agents who stole a half-million dollars from the government.

Vid. Alt.: *The FBI Story*, starring Jimmy Stewart in an episodic tribute to J. Edgar Hoover and the Bureau.

WIND (1992). Matthew Modine, Jennifer Grey. Adventure (a dozen or so profanities, some mild expletives, sexual relationships outside marriage). Lovers involved in the running of America's Cup. There's a thread of a story line holding the racing scenes together, but the film's energy is only evident during the ocean sequences. The cinematography is often breathtaking, even when you're not sure what the competitors are doing. If the writers had trimmed about 20 minutes of the land-locked scenes and replaced them with clarity about sailboat racing, they might have had a great film.

Vid. Alt. featuring romance and adventure on the high seas: *The African Queen* (1951). Bogart and Hepburn as a mismatched pair traveling downriver in a small boat, attempting to escape the Germans.

THE WITCHES (1990). Anjelica Huston. Adventure - PG13 (witchcraft). Fantasy about witches out to destroy all children.

Vid. Alt.: *Babes in Toyland* (1934 version with Laurel and Hardy). Good battles evil in this lovely musical fantasy.

WITHOUT YOU I'M NOTHING (1990). Sandra Bernhard. Rated R. This one-woman show takes shots at the idiosyncrasies of society, but like most comics of today who feed off these foibles, Bernhard offers no solutions.

For a funny one-person **Vid. Alt.**, try *Bill Cosby, Himself* (1981). One-man show dealing with raising children and marriage. His routine on dentists rates up there with Abbott and Costello's "Who's On First?" (Caution: a few expletives.)

CHAPTER III

VIDEO SUGGESTIONS
FILMS FOR ALL FAMILY MEMBERS

The movies listed in this chapter are considered 3- or 4-star films by most film critics. Although these motion pictures will not bombard your senses with lots of bad language, extreme violence or sexual situations, very few films are made with the concept of preserving family values. So if you find something objectionable, might I suggest you put the VCR on pause and discuss the offending issue with the family. In many cases you'll find this practice to be the best part of movie viewing.

VIDEOS FOR CHILDREN
(Adults will enjoy as well)
Caution: Many fables contain witches, ghosts or sorcery. If you should see some element in a movie that might be confusing to young minds, take the opportunity to discuss it with them.

THE ABSENT-MINDED PROFESSOR (1961). Fred MacMurray and Tommy Kirk star in this Disney classic about a college professor who invents "flubber," a substance that enables people to fly.

THE ADVENTURES OF MILO & OTIS (1989). Rated G. Great adventure film starring animals, with Dudley Moore serving as narrator. Highest grossing film ever in Japan. Little kids and their parents will adore it.

ALMOST ANGELS (1962). Disney story of two mischievous boys who become friends in the Vienna Boys Choir.

THE AMAZING MR. BLUNDEN (1972). A family picture about a ghost who helps two abused children.

THE ARISTOCATS (1970). Disney animated film with voices of Eva Gabor, Phil Harris, Scatman Crothers and many other character actors.

THE BANK DICK (1940). W. C. Fields at his very best as an inept bank guard.

BEETHOVEN (1992). Charles Grodin, Dean Jones

(against type as the bad guy). Comedy - PG (1 vulgar expression for which the culprit is reprimanded). Escapist fare about a St. Bernard eluding a mad doctor who wants to use puppies for target practice. Soon, the mischievous canine transforms the mundane life of a dysfunctional family. In spite of disapproving critics, both kids and their parents seem to enjoy this film.

THE BOY WHO COULD FLY (1986). Fantasy, rated PG (two expletives). A young girl moves next door to an autistic boy who believes he can fly. A moving fable parents will enjoy viewing with their kids. Lucy Deakins, Fred Savage.

THE BRAVE LITTLE TOASTER (1987). Creative animated story of household appliances that come to life when no one's home. They share several adventures as they go into the world searching for their owner. The talents of several Saturday Night Live alumni make this silly tale a pleasure for adults as well. Positive messages about friendship, loyalty and self-sacrifice.

CARTOON ALL-STARS TO THE RESCUE. This anti-drug video, which ran on all the networks simultaneously several months ago, is now at your local video store. Truly an effective weapon against a destructive force that no child is too young to learn about. It's excellent. Adults will enjoy it as well. Good for starting a conversation with kids.

THE GREAT MOUSE DETECTIVE (1986). Disney animation, rated G (the lead smokes a pipe; you might want to discuss the ills of smoking with impressionable tykes). A fun adventure about Basil of Baker Street, a brilliant mouse who lives under Sherlock Holmes' apartment.

HAPPY BIRTHDAY, BUGS: 50 LOONEY YEARS. With guests Milton Berle, Bill Cosby, John Goodman, and, of course, Bugs Bunny and all his pals. Don't kid yourself...you'll enjoy it more than the kids.

HOMEWARD BOUND (1993). Disney animal tale about two dogs and a cat separated from their human "pets." Rated G, with voices of Don Ameche, Michael J. Fox and Sally Field. A joy to watch with the kids.

HONEY, I BLEW UP THE KID (1992). Rick Moranis, Marcia Strassman. Comedy - PG (a few scenes may be a little too intense for very small children. After all, it's not every day they see a 100-foot two-year-old). A nutty inventor accidentally exposes his son to a ray gun that enlarges objects. Soon he, his wife and the National Guard are attempting to stop a giant toddler from destroying Las Vegas. A one-joke movie, not as fun as *Honey, I Shrunk the Kids* (which is a good **Vid. Alt.**), but wholesome enough for the whole family.

HONEY, I SHRUNK THE KIDS (1989). Rated PG (a few scenes may be too scary for very small children). Most kids will love this one. There are lots of special effects and excitement as a scientist's children are accidentally shrunk by his new invention. When they get put out with the trash, it's a real adventure trying to get back home—across their backyard.

THE JOURNEY OF NATTY GANN (1985). Meredith Salenger, John Cusack. A teenage girl travels across the country searching for her father. She is befriended by an unusual young man and a wolf! A Disney classic.

THE JUNGLE BOOK (1942). Kipling tale of a boy raised by animals. The Disney 1967 animated musical version seems to be more enjoyable for little ones.

THE NEVER ENDING STORY, Part II. Rated PG. A fable most kids 8-13 will enjoy with its adventure and special effects. Teaches sacrifices, honor, friendship and courage.

DALMATIANS (Disney, 1961). Tale of a villainess who wants to turn puppies into fur coats. Of course our heroes put an end to that. It is a charming and—compared to today's standards—gentle story the whole family can enjoy.

THE RESCUERS (1977). Disney cartoon - G. An all-mouse Rescue Aid Society. Witty script is also helped along by the voices of Bob Newhart, Eva Gabor and many other Disney regulars.

RESCUERS DOWN UNDER (1990). Disney-animated tale of a group of animals out to rescue a kidnapped boy. Voices of Bob Newhart, Eva Gabor, John Candy, and George C. Scott.

SONG OF THE SOUTH (1946). Considered by many as Disney's best film. Story of young boy's friendship with a loving old black man on his grandmother's plantation. Great animation and Oscar-winning music.

THE THIEF OF BAGHDAD (1940 version). Sabu. Outstanding special effects for the time, and a very imaginative script about a young merchant who frees a genie.

WHITE FANG (1990). Klaus Maria Brandauer, Ethan Hawke. A young man befriends a wolf in this Jack London tale. Beautifully photographed in Alaska.

VIDEOS FOR TEENS

ALAN & NAOMI (1992). Lukas Haas, Vanessa Zaoni. Drama - PG (perhaps a little too intense for very small children, but contains no bad language or off-color humor). Very touching tale of a young boy helping a traumatized girl who witnessed her father's murder by the Nazis. Teaches responsibility and compassion. Good performances.

DARK HORSE (1991). Ed Begley, Jr., Mimi Rodgers, Ari Meyers. Drama. A rebellious teenager learning about responsibility and commitment when she is sentenced to working on a horse farm. Rated PG for a dozen or so mild expletives. I bring it to your attention because I believe the positive messages outweigh the mild language.

THE GIRL OF THE LIMBERLOST (1990). Annette O'Toole, Joanna Cassidy, Heather Fairfield. A young girl is determined to get an education in 1908 rural Indiana.

JACOB HAVE I LOVED. Bridget Fonda, Jenny Robertson. A shy, insecure teenager comes to grips with the resentment she feels for her twin sister. Sensitive story dealing with sibling rivalry.

NO SECOND CHANCE. A dynamic look at teens and the HIV virus. For nearest distributor, contact Jeremiah Films at (800) 633-0869.

VIDEOS FOR THE ENTIRE FAMILY

ANNE OF AVONLEA (1987). Engaging sequel to *Anne of Green Gables*.

ANNE OF GREEN GABLES (1985). A superb cast headed by Colleen Dewhurst, Richard Farnsworth and Megan Follows. One of the few instances where the film lives up to the quality of the book. Not to be missed.

THE BOY WITH GREEN HAIR (1948). Dean Stockwell, Pat O'Brien. A fable about a war orphan who becomes an outcast when his hair turns green. Although when made the film spoke of European children whose parents were killed in the war, today's audience gets a poignant message about the discrimination children with AIDS must face.

FOR ALL MANKIND (1989). Rated G. Documentary the whole family can view. A beautifully made film about Neil Armstrong's flight to the moon.

FORBIDDEN PLANET (1956). Walter Pidgeon, Leslie Nielsen, Anne Francis. Intelligent sci-fi film about space explorers landing on a planet ruled by one man and an evil force. Plot derived from Shakespeare's *The Tempest*.

THE GIRL WHO SPELLED FREEDOM (1986). Hard to find, but worth the effort. Wayne Rodgers and Mary Kay Place star in this made-for-TV story of a Christian family who take in a Cambodian refugee. Not only does the teenager learn English, but she goes on to win a national spelling bee. Theme: With love and perseverance anything is possible. Strong performances and a literate script make this a pleasure for kids and adults.

LITTLE HEROES. Based on a true story. Begins slowly, but it's an inspiring tale of a poor girl and her beloved dog, and their effect on the local community. Presents courage, responsibility, family values and messages such as "It's what you are, not what you have, that counts." Stars Raeanin Simpson.

LOVE LEADS THE WAY (1984). True story of Morris Frank, who started the Seeing Eye Dog Foundation and got bills passed okaying seeing eye dogs on buses, in restaurants, etc. Very moving. Timothy Bottoms.

NATIONAL VELVET (1945). Family drama about a young girl who disguises herself as a boy in order to compete in the English Grand National Steeplechase. Elizabeth Taylor, Mickey Rooney.

NO TIME FOR SERGEANTS (1958). Andy Griffith,

Don Knotts. Want a really good laugh? This is full of them. Andy's a country boy drafted into the army. Myron McCormick as the frustrated sergeant is outstanding.

THE NUTTY PROFESSOR (1963). Jerry Lewis in top form as the lovable Professor Julius Kept and his alter ego, Buddy Love. A comic version of Jekyll & Hyde with Lewis providing some of his greatest sight gags.

THE RED PONY (1949). A John Steinbeck novel about a boy and his horse. Great Aaron Copland score. Robert Mitchum is outstanding as the wise ranch hand. Film teaches responsibility.

Hope and Crosby's ROAD PICTURES are now on video. *The Road to Singapore, Zanzibar, Morocco, Utopia, Rio, Bali, Hong Kong.* The boys get around, and always seem to run into Dorothy Lamour. Each contains enough slapstick to keep the kids interested and enough droll one-liners to put adults in stitches. *Bali* and *Morocco* are my favs.

SHIPWRECKED (1990). Disney adventure reminiscent of *Swiss Family Robinson.* PG (man is killed by the villain at the beginning of the story). A shipwrecked boy and his mates protect a treasure from pirates. Teaches responsibility and commitment. Well made for kids, with great locations and musical score.

SOUNDER (1972). Paul Winfield, Cicely Tyson, Kevin Hooks. Rated G. Stirring story of a black sharecropper's family during the Depression. Nominated for best picture that year along with the lead actors. Truly marvelous.

THE SOUND OF MUSIC (1965). Julie Andrews, Christopher Plummer. Oscar-winning film based on the lives of the Von Trapps, a talented musical family, with the children seeking their distant father's love.

THAT'S ENTERTAINMENT, Parts 1 and 2. (1974, 1976). The perfect musicals for those of us who love the artistry of MGM's stable of stars yet hate the corny story lines that so often accompanied the '30s and '40s musical comedies. No silly scenarios here, just Astaire, Rogers and about a hundred other luminaries doing what they do best.

TOM THUMB (1958). Stars Russ Tamblyn and is

based on the Grimm fairy tale. Features Peter Sellers and Terry Thomas, and great music from Peggy Lee and Sonny Burke. Oscar-winning special effects.

TREASURE ISLAND. This Robert Louis Stevenson classic has been remade several times. Most critics agree that the 1934 version with Wallace Berry and the 1950 version with Robert Newton are the best. Both are available on video.

A TREE GROWS IN BROOKLYN (1945 version with James Dunn, Dorothy McGuire). A four-star film about turn-of-the-century family life in a New York tenement.

THE VOLCANO WATCHERS, a PBS home video about scientists who put their lives on the line in order to discover more about nature at its most volatile.

WHERE THE RED FERN GROWS (1974). Heart-warming story full of charm and lessons of responsibility. Stars James Whitmore and Stewart Peterson.

WILD HEARTS CAN'T BE BROKEN (1991). Gabrielle Anwar is outstanding as the young girl determined to become a carnival stunt rider.

YOURS, MINE AND OURS (1968). Lucille Ball, Henry Fonda. Based on a true story of a widow with eight kids who marries a widower with ten. Lucy is very funny in this film for the whole family.

Keep receiving *The Movie Reporter Newsletter* in order to maintain an updated monthly list of quality video alternatives for your family. A subscription card is attached at the end of the book. Subscription price $15.00 per year (limited offer). Central Christian Publications, P O Box 7178, Thousand Oaks, CA 91359.

VIDEOS FOR MORE MATURE VIEWERS

ADAM (1983). Daniel J. Travanti, JoBeth Williams. Horrifying true story of a couple's search for their kidnapped child. Gritty, moving script by Allan Leicht.

ALL ABOUT EVE (1950). Bette Davis at her best as a sophisticated actress at odds with her scheming protege. Winner of six Oscars, including Best

Picture and Best Screenplay. Witty dialogue and sharp performances make this a 4-star picture.

ALL MY SONS (1948). Edward G. Robinson, Burt Lancaster. Compelling Arthur Miller story about a dysfunctional family.

ANSEL ADAMS. Documentary on one of the greatest photographers America has brought forth. Sixty minutes in length, it is full of his spirit and artistry.

AVALON (1990). Armin Mueller Stahl, Elizabeth Perkins. PG (a few profanities). Superb filmmaking about Polish immigrants who settle in Baltimore in 1914. I bring this to your attention because of its strong statement about the importance of the family. It's a beautifully photographed, emotionally charged film that should have received an Oscar nomination.

CABIN IN THE SKY (1943). Ethel Waters, Lena Horne, Eddie "Rochester" Anderson. Musical comedy. Fable about faith and devotion. Ingratiating performance by Waters, and several moving musical numbers.

CHARADE (1963). Cary Grant, Audrey Hepburn. Amusing mystery with Grant at his elegant best, aiding Audrey in search of a missing fortune. Adding to the fun—Walter Matthau, James Coburn and George Kennedy. One of Henry Mancini's best scores.

CITIZEN KANE (1941). Drama. At the age of 25, Orson Welles starred in, directed, and co-wrote what may be the best film ever made. Along with his cinematographer, editor and other pioneering technicians, Welles brought many innovations to the movie world. With the use of lighting, camera angles, and brilliant direction, Welles tells the rise-to-power story of a William Randolph Hearst-like publisher.

CRY, THE BELOVED COUNTRY (1951). Sidney Poitier. A British film about the struggle between races in South Africa. Poignant without bombarding your senses with today's screen profanity and violence.

DAMIEN, THE LEPER PRIEST (1980, made for TV). Ken Howard in a true story of a priest dedicated to a leper colony. Not a great movie, but a positive portrayal of a man of the cloth, without any preaching.

THE DEAD (1987). Drama. Anjelica Huston and a largely Irish cast star in this story of a lively holiday dinner party set in Ireland, circa 1904. John Huston's last film isn't for everybody, but the laid-back atmospheric study of the morals of the day is a gentle reminder of the late director's vast abilities.

DESK SET (1957). A bit dated, but Spencer Tracy, Katharine Hepburn and a trenchant script make this comedy a must-see. No one has ever topped the coupling of Tracy and Hepburn.

THE DEVIL AT 4 O'CLOCK (1961). Adventure on a tropic island doomed by a menacing volcano. Spencer Tracy and Frank Sinatra star as a dispirited priest and a sarcastic convict at odds with one another and God until they pull together to rescue villagers from the erupting volcano.

DISRAELI (1929). George Arliss won an Oscar for his performance as the great statesman and British prime minister.

DOUBLE INDEMNITY (1944). Barbara Stanwyck, Fred MacMurray, Edward G. Robinson (outstanding). Adroit script about a couple planning to murder her husband.

EL CID (1961). Charlton Heston, Sophia Loren. Historical drama/romance about the legendary hero who drove the Moors from Spain. Great spectacle, with a literate script, a lovely score, and arguably the most beautiful woman ever to appear on the silver screen.

ENCHANTED APRIL (1992). Joan Plowright, Polly Walker. A delightful fable about four women in the 1920s escaping their repressed lifestyles in London by renting a castle in Portofino. They soon discover the estate has a magical effect on all those who stay there. Witty dialogue, dreamy cinematography, and savory performances. At last, a PG film with no sexual activity, profane language, violence or religion-bashing. A romantic comedy that nourishes the spirit.

THE FAR COUNTRY (1986). Michael York, Sigrid Thornton. Drama. A doctor who served in the German army escapes to Australia at the end of the war. There he has to overcome prejudice and a possible prison sentence when he exposes his profession in order to perform a life-saving operation. Rated PG (3 or 4 expletives, one violent murder early on).

FATHER OF THE BRIDE (1991). Steve Martin, Kimberly Williams. Comedy - PG (one crude joke about the use of a condom). Truly a sensitive, often hilarious look at a father dealing with his daughter's upcoming marriage. Martin is no Spencer Tracy, but he is credible. Newcomer Kimberly Williams is perfect. And what a pleasure to be able to bring to your attention a recent film with no violence, language or sexual situations.

THE FILMS OF 1939: Classics—All! Perhaps the most prolific year for vintage movies. Here are just a few. *Beau Geste, Dark Victory, Destry Rides Again, Four Feathers, Golden Boy, Gone With The Wind, Goodbye Mr. Chips, Hound of the Baskervilles, Hunchback of Notre Dame, Mr. Smith Goes To Washington, Ninotchka, Private Lives of Elizabeth & Essex, Stagecoach, Wizard of Oz, The Women, Wuthering Heights, You Can't Cheat An Honest Man,* and *Young Mr. Lincoln.* And only one expletive in the bunch! Here's a bit of trivia. Do you remember the film and the character who said the first curse that truly was heard around the world? (Rhett Butler in *Gone With The Wind*).

FOXFIRE (1987). Jessica Tandy, Hume Cronym and John Denver. A Hallmark Hall of Fame presentation about an elderly woman unable to leave her farm because the ghost of her late husband resides there. Amusing, dramatic, poignant. Tandy won an Emmy.

GENTLEMAN'S AGREEMENT (1947). Gregory Peck. A writer posing as a Jew discovers anti-Semitism.

GONE WITH THE WIND (1939). Clark Gable, Vivian Leigh. Storytelling at its best.

HIGH SOCIETY (1956). Musical version of the 1940 classic *The Philadelphia Story*. Frank Sinatra, Bing Crosby, Grace Kelly, Louis Armstrong are featured in this romantic remake, along with the music of Cole Porter.

THE INCIDENT (1990). Walter Matthau, Barnard Hughes, Susan Blakely. A Hallmark Hall of Fame presentation about a country lawyer defending a German soldier in a murder trial during WWII.

INDIANA JONES AND THE LAST CRUSADE. (1988). Rated PG (lots of violence, one profanity, for which the culprit is immediately punished). Funny, thrilling. Sean Connery and Harrison Ford are terrific as father and son searching for the Holy Grail.

THE JERICHO MILE (1979). TV movie starring Peter Strauss as a prison lifer who attempts to become the world's fastest runner. Notable script.

JUDGMENT AT NUREMBERG (1961). Drama. A U.S. judge presides over wartime criminal trials. Outstanding all-star cast includes Spencer Tracy, Maximillian Schell, Burt Lancaster, Judy Garland, Montgomery Cliff. Oscars went to Schell and screen writer Abby Mann. Well crafted by director Stanley Kramer.

LAURA (1944). Another four-star classic, starring Gene Tierney, Dana Andrews and Clifton Webb. A superb romantic murder mystery.

LAURENCE OLIVIER was renown not just as an actor, but for his producing and directing abilities, as well as being perhaps the finest interpreter of Shakespearean roles. For those of us who have labored through the Bard's tragedies, Olivier helped make the meaning clear and helped us to understand how a gorgeous use of language gave a richer meaning to story-listening.

Most people acquainted with his stage work comprehend his fame as the world's greatest actor. On film, Olivier's presence could be more of a hit and miss. However, the following are excellent films and a prestigious showcase for a truly remarkable actor: *Wuthering Heights, Hamlet, Henry V, Richard II, The Prince and the Showgirl, The Entertainer, Rebecca.*

LILIES OF THE FIELD (1963). Drama. Sidney Poitier was the first black man to win a best-actor Oscar, for his wonderful performance as a handyman who helps build a chapel for an order of nuns.

THE LONG WALK HOME (1990). Sissy Spacek, Whoopie Goldberg. PG (adult subjects, 3 or 4 obscenities). Two women who sacrifice much during the beginning of the civil rights movement. A very important film that not only exposes racism but gives examples of justice.

LOVE IS NEVER SILENT (1985). Another Emmy winner featuring Mare Winningham as a woman torn between building a life of her own and remaining with her deaf parents, who depend on her as their link to the outside world.

THE MAN WHO CAME TO DINNER (1941). Monty Wooley, Bette Davis. When a pompous man injures himself in front of a family of good Samaritans, he finds himself their houseguest. Unfortunately for the good souls, he begins to drive them crazy with his boring stories and weird friends. Very funny. Highly recommended.

MARTY (1955). Oscar-winning writer Paddy Chayefsky provides an erudite script, with Ernest Borgnine giving an Oscar-winning performance as a middle-aged, lonely man who finds love. Best Picture of that year.

MASADA (1984). Peter O'Toole and Peter Strauss give formidable performances in a superior TV movie about he battle at Masada between the Jews and Romans. (Caution—some violence, especially during the opening scenes.)

MGM: WHEN THE LION ROARS (1992). The story behind perhaps the greatest of the movie studios.

MR. NORTH (1988). Robert Mitchum, Lauren Bacall, Anjelica Huston. Rated PG (one objectionable phrase). magical young man enters the lives of the idle rich in 1926 Newport, RI. Beautifully photographed, great cast; and, if you want a happy ending, this is the one for you.

MURDER MOST FOUL, *Murder Ahoy, Murder She Said* and *Murder At the Gallop*. Agatha Christie's super sleuth, iss Marple, has never been more aptly portrayed than by Oscar-winning English actress Margaret Rutherford. Finally, the mid-'60s British film series is available on video. Brew a cup of Earl Gray on a stormy afternoon and enjoy a marvelous who-done-it.

ON THE BEACH (1959). Gregory Peck, Ava Gardner, Fred Astaire (in a fine dramatic role). Adroit script abut survivors of nuclear war awaiting the end of the world. This film is a terrific example of adult subject matter, including romance, effectively handled with discretion.

ON THE WATERFRONT (1954). Marlon Brando, Eva Marie Saint, Rod Steiger. Winner of eight Academy Awards, daling with New York's crime-ridden harbor docks. Another excellent example of romance, emotional stress and vice masterfully told without the language and brutality associated with today's movies.

THE PISTOL: THE BIRTH OF A LEGEND (1991). G-rated film about the life of Pete Maravich. A very inspirational biography, suitable for the entire family.

PLACES IN THE HEART (1984). Sally Field, Danny Glover. Rated PG (some mild language, implied adulterous affair). In spite of these few negatives, the film contains an award-winning performance by Sally Field, an uplifting moral, and one of the most moving endings ever filmed.

THE PRIVATE LIFE OF HENRY VIII (1933). A 4-star adaptation of the 16th-century monarch. Stars Charles Laughton, Robert Donat and Merle Oberon.

QUARTET (1949). Four short stories eloquently written and introduced by Somerset Maugham. Not to be mistaken with the 1981 film of the same name. Also ask for the sequel: **TRIO**.

ROCKET GIBRALTAR (1988). Rated PG (a few expletives). Burt Lancaster and a very capable supporting cast enliven this heartwarming story of a family reunion to celebrate the patriarch's 77th birthday. Really nice story of children connecting with their grandfather.

SARAH, PLAIN AND TALL (1991). Glenn Close, Christopher Walken. A Hallmark Hall of Fame story. Stars Glenn Close as a woman in the 1880s who answers an ad to share a life on a Kansas farm. Nominated for nine Emmys. Highly recommended.

SAVING GRACE (1986). Tom Conti. Com/Dra, rated PG (2 expletives). A pope feeling out of touch with the people and wondering if he has any real effect outside the Vatican walls, ventures out incognito to a small spiritless town. It moves slowly in some places, but it has great heart and reveals how, with God's help, one man can make a difference.

THE SCARLET AND THE BLACK (1983). Made-for-TV true story of a priest (Gregory Peck) who harbored allied POW escapees and the Nazi official (Christopher Plummer) who tries to catch him. The film is a bit long (155 min.) but the message contained at the end of the picture should not be missed. A true example of Jesus' compassion will help remind each of us to love our enemies.

SINGING IN THE RAIN (1952). Most everybody is familiar with Gene Kelly's version of "Singing in the Rain" (alone worth the rental price). But there are several great numbers in this film, including perhaps the funniest musical number ever filmed—Donald O'Connor's "Make Em Laugh." Good story, fabulous dancing, and memorable tunes make this the granddad of musicals.

STARLIGHT HOTEL (1987). Drama, rated PG (one profanity). Late 1920s in New Zealand, a troubled 13-year-old girl runs away to find her father who has left in search of work. During her sojourn, the girl meets up with a man running from the law.

THE SUNDOWNERS (1960). Robert Mitchum, Peter Ustinov, Deborah Kerr star in this entertaining tale of sheepherders in Australia. Romantic, humorous, moving.

TENDER MERCIES (1983). Robert Duvall. Drama, rated PG (a few obscenities from our hero until a Christian woman has an effect on his life). A country singer on the skids gets his life together with the help of a religious widow. Oscars went to Duvall and writer Horton Foote.

TO SLEEP WITH ANGER (1990). Danny Glover. Comedy/drama - PG (several obscenities). Eerie tale of a mysterious man who subtly manipulates family and friends.

THE TRIP TO BOUNTIFUL (1985). Geraldine Page. Simple but well-told story of discontented widow who decides to make a last pilgrimage to her childhood home. Page won Best Actress for her wonderfully textured performance. The beautiful rendition of "Softly and Tenderly" by Christian performer Cynthia Clawson is worth the rental price. PG (a couple of expletives).

TWO WEEKS IN ANOTHER TOWN (1962). Kirk Douglas, Edward G. Robinson, Clair Trevor. The trials and tribulations of a group making a movie in Rome. (Adult subject matter.)

THE WANNESS CONFERENCE (1986). Not rated. German film with subtitles. True account of the infamous meeting in Berlin (1942) by Nazi leaders to discuss the "final solution to the Jewish problem." Based on stenographer's notes, the film's length matches the event's actual running time. This is a very well made and horrifying story—lest we forget.

WEST SIDE STORY (1961). Romeo & Juliet set to music and ballet, amid 1950s New York City gangs. I don't know how they did it, but it works. Music by Leonard Bernstein (our Mozart), directed by veteran Robert Wise, and winner of 10 Oscars.

CHRISTMAS CLASSICS

THE BISHOP'S WIFE (1947). A debonair angel attempts to help a frustrated pastor and his neglected wife. Cary Grant, Loretta Young, David Niven.

A CHARLIE BROWN CHRISTMAS (1965). A perfect animated tale by Charles Schultz with the "Peanuts" gang searching for the true meaning of Christmas. Great dialogue, charismatic voice performances and an award-winning jazzy score by Vince Guaraldi. And how often do you hear cartoon heroes quoting from the gospel of Luke, proclaiming the Christ-child as the Messiah?

When it comes to the famous Dickens tale, here are three of the best renditions: **A CHRISTMAS CAROL** (1951) starring Alastair Sim; **A CHRISTMAS CAROL** (1984) with George C. Scott; and the musical version, **SCROOGE** (1970), with Albert Finney. Each a well-acted parable with regard to redemption.

CHRISTMAS EVE (1986). Loretta Young, Ron Leibman, Trevor Howard head a seasoned cast in an account of an elderly woman trying to bring her grandchildren and their father back together. Young had not made a film in 23 years, yet proved she was still glamorous and gifted.

A CHRISTMAS WITHOUT SNOW (1980). Made-for-TV about a woman (Michael Learned) who becomes involved with the members of her church choir and its perfectionist director (John Houseman).

THE GATHERING (1977). with Ed Asner, Maureen Stapleton. This Emmy-winning TV movie focuses on a dying man's efforts to reunite his family. It reinforces the importance of family and presents positive Christian images including a believable prayer, the scripture reading of Jesus' birth, and a child's baptism. Forget the sequel.

THE GREATEST ADVENTURE—THE NATIVITY. Hanna-Barbera's animated video series explores the lives of biblical heroes including this version of the birth of Christ. Entertaining and educational. Also in the collection: the Easter story, as seen through the eyes of three young visitors from the 20th century.

IT'S A WONDERFUL LIFE (1946). I know, I know, we've all seen it a million times, but won't you agree with me that it is one of the most important films Hollywood ever produced? James Stewart is given the opportunity to see what his community would have been like if he had never been born. He reminds us that we touch so many lives and can have a real influence on those lives. Full of Christian symbolism, *It's a Wonderful Life* reinforces the belief that our compassion and responsibility do make a difference in the lives of those with whom we come in contact. Director Frank Capra has given the world a great gift with this Christmas classic.

JESUS OF NAZARETH (1977). Franco Zeffirelli's epic production of the life of Christ. Considered by many as the best film about the Son of Man, *Jesus of Nazareth* is acclaimed for its thorough biblical and historical research. A very moving and spiritual experience, with many memorable performances including those of Robert Powell, Anne Bancroft, Ernest Borgnine, and Laurence Olivier. Its length (371 min.) will take several evenings to digest, but I highly recommend the effort.

THE LITTLE DRUMMER BOY (1968). The very moving seasonal song comes to animated life with the capable voices of Greer Garson, Jose Ferrer, and Teddy Eccles. Puts present-giving in perspective.

MR. MAGOO'S CHRISTMAS CAROL (1962). You put Jim Backus together with Dickens' timeless classic, then add the Broadway talents of Jule Styne and Bob Merrill and you're bound to have entertainment fit for the kid in all of us. Now don't tell anybody this, but I've watched this little gem each year since it first premiered—once or twice in July!

THE OTHER WISEMAN. Also animated, this Christmas classic has been adapted for children. It tells the story of a man seeking the birthplace of Jesus but, because of his duty to others, is delayed in the desert for 33 years only to see the Saviour as He is being crucified. Hard to find; check your local Christian bookstore.

THE STABLE BOY'S CHRISTMAS (1979). Danielle Brisebois, Darleen Carr, Sparky Marcus and several of Hollywood's best character actors lend their talents to this Emmy-winning 27-minute TV special concerning a selfish young girl who learns a great lesson about the Christmas season from a figurine that comes to life. Soon we are transported to the night of Christ's birth where we witness the Savior's effect on the people of Bethlehem. Not in the same league as the others mentioned in this category, but like *The Little Drummer Boy*, it helps put present-giving in perspective.

THREE GODFATHERS (1948). John Wayne, Pedro Armendariz, Harry Carey, Jr. Three outlaws, running from a posse, come across a dying woman and her newborn baby. The symbolism between the Christ-child and this new foundling has a redemptive effect on the three bandits. Sincere performances, beautiful cinematography and the skillful direction of John Ford highlight this insightful western.

NOT YET ON VIDEO

THE HOLLY AND THE IVY. Sir Ralph Richardson heads a capable English cast in this story of a dysfunctional family brought together in a remote Norfolk rectory. This well-acted British film is not yet on video. It usually airs at around 3:00 in the morning on local TV stations during the Christmas season. Might I suggest you VCR it! It's worth the effort.

CHAPTER IV

INSPIRATIONAL VIDEOS

Most people agree, the spirit of man is something that needs to be nourished. Many are searching for answers, for guidance, for faith.

Although "religious" movies have a bad reputation—often justified—there are exceptions. Most Christian bookstores are now offering a large selection of quality videos aiming to fulfill the enjoyment and spiritual needs of your entire family.

For readers who have not made a decision to accept Christ Jesus as Lord and Savior, override your preconceived notions and visit a Christian bookstore. Contrary to what the news media would have you believe, the Christian community is not fairly represented by a few corrupt T.V. evangelists, but by a people who follow the teachings of a man who commanded us to "love God and to love one another" (Matthew 22:36-40). The bookstore employees will be glad to help you find material that answers your questions about the Christian faith.

COMEDY

GOD VIEWS. Gospel Films. Curt Cloninger presents comic sketches on our misconceptions of God. Length: 42 minutes. Great to show to kids (8-12) while discussing who God is and how much He loves us.

THE GOSPEL BLIMP (1967). Gospel Films. Dated, but often humorous look at religious organizations that turn sharing the gospel into a business.

MARK LOWRY: MY FIRST COMEDY VIDEO. Word. An insightful stand-up comedy routine. Highly recommended.

WHITCOMB'S WAR (1988). Patrick Parkhurst. A satire about a young pastor battling a hard-nosed businessman and the "powers of darkness" from trying to control a town.

DOCUMENTARY

CHILDREN AT RISK. Focus on the Family offers this 60-minute film concerned with how you and your church can protect children against anti-family influences. Available for church groups on a rental basis. For more information on this well-made film, contact Focus on the Family Educational Resources at 1-800-932-9123 and ask for the Christian film distributor nearest you.

JESUS. Campus Crusade presents a 2-hour documentary on the life of Christ.

THE MESSIAH. 30-minute documentary on the life of Christ. An entertaining, educational tool.

MOTHER TERESA (1983—80 minutes). Hard to find, well-made documentary about a woman who has given her life to Christ. If you are looking for an inspirational tape, I cannot recommend this film enough. It will uplift and encourage you to see Christ's example of love and sacrifice at work. It is not a salute to one woman or church, but rather evidence that Christ's teachings are being put to use and making a difference in our world. I have never been so moved or challenged by a movie.

DRAMA

BEN HUR (1959). Charlton Heston, directed by William Wyler. (Contains no swearing or nudity, but some violence.) Ben Hur won 11 Oscars including Best Picture and Best Actor. Story of a noble man forced into slavery and the effect Christ had on his life. Very moving ending, and the exciting chariot race is among the all-time great action scenes.

CHARIOTS OF FIRE. Winner of (1981) Best Picture about Eric Liddell, a devout Scottish missionary who ran in the 1924 Olympics. Worth seeing a second time. Ian Charleson, Ben Cross.

FURY TO FREEDOM (The Word For Today-New Direction). Well-made true story of a troubled youth who inherits the same abusive traits as his father, until he accepts Jesus Christ as his Saviour. Erik Jacobson wrote and directed this powerful story that both young people and adults will relate to. Highly recommended.

GREATER THAN THOU. Evangelical Films presents this powerful drama about a pregnant teenager considering abortion. Themes discussed: family communications, sanctity of life, and the cost of discipleship.

THE HIDING PLACE (1975). Jeannette Clift stars as Corrie Ten Boom, who worked with the underground during World War II, helping to save the lives of many Jews. Imprisoned herself in one of Germany's worst concentration camps, Corrie learned "there is no pit so deep that He is not deeper still." A moving film about compassion and forgiveness.

HUDSON TAYLOR. Ken Anderson Films' dramatic true story of the first evangelist to go into mainland China.

INN OF THE SIXTH HAPPINESS (1958). Ingrid Bergman. Based on a true story of a missionary who leads a group of children on a perilous journey in pre-WW2 China. Contains the most moving conversion I've seen in the movies, as we witness change in a man's life due to this courageous woman's example. It reminds the Christian viewer that our lifestyle does greatly affect others.

JESUS OF NAZARETH (1977 - CBS/Fox Video). Franco Zeffirelli's epic production of the life of Christ can also be found at your local Christian bookstore. Considered by many as the best film about Christ, *Jesus of Nazareth* is acclaimed for its thorough biblical and historical research. A very moving and spiritual experience, with many memorable performances. Its length (371 min.) will take several evenings to digest, but I highly recommend the effort. Robert Powell heads an all-star cast.

MARK IV. Presents a top rental series on the tribulation and last times. The series begins with *A Thief in the Night, A Distant Thunder, Image of the Beast* and *Prodigal Planet*. This is not this reviewer's favorite series. I found these films to be extremely outdated, but there are some very effective statements about the future and, as I say, they remain top rentals. People are very concerned with the role of the Christian in the last times. These films attempt to take a serious look at this provocative subject.

NO GREATER LOVE. Once an alcoholic, wife abuser and murderer, Ricardo Garcia becomes one of Mexico's outstanding Christian leaders. Harvest Productions presentation adapted from the book *Martyred in Mexico*.

PEACE CHILD. True story of missionaries Don and Carol Richardson, who travel to a remote jungle inhabited by some of the world's most primitive people. When war breaks out, a chief offers his infant son as the means of bringing peace. A powerful evangelical tool, *Peace Child* is a welcome addition to your home or church library. For information concerning this and other great gospel videos, write to Gospel Films, P O Box 455, Muskegon, Michigan 49443.

THE PROSECUTOR. A drama debating the evidence for and against Jesus' resurrection in a modern trial setting. Features Jerry Houser, Bob Pierce and Phil Boatwright. A Gospel Films release.

THE ROBE (1953). Based on the Lloyd C. Douglas novel about a Roman centurion who wins Christ's robe in a dice game. Soon his life, and that of his slave, are changed as they discover Jesus to be the Saviour of the World. We see Jesus through the use of long shots and camera angles that focus the attention not on an actor portraying Christ, but on the people who came into His presence. This method was effectively used, giving the story a great dignity.

Richard Burton was nominated for an Oscar, but Victor Mature steals the picture with a moving performance as the converted slave, Demetrius. The depiction of the early church and the life-changing power of our Lord make this film worth viewing.

THE SCARLET AND THE BLACK (1983 made-for-TV movie). True story of a priest (Gregory Peck) who harbored allied POW escapees and the Nazi official (Christopher Plummer) who tries to catch him. The film is a bit long (155 min.) but the message contained at the end of the picture should not be missed. A true example of Christ's compassion will help remind each of us to love our enemies.

SEEDS FOR THE HARVEST. True story produced by Focus on the Family about a man who, much like Noah, steps out on faith in order to obey God, in spite of the unbelief of others. Available for rent from Mike Adkins Ministries, (618) 932-3782 or (618) 932-3556.

SHADOWLANDS (1985). Joss Ackland, Claire Bloom. Award-winning film spotlighting the friendship and eventual marriage of English author C. S. Lewis and an American woman who discovers she is dying. A lovely film which deals with the loss of a loved one.

ST. JOHN IN EXILE. Dean Jones stars in this one-man show about the Apostle John. D.J. Productions.

KIDS

ADVENTURES IN ODYSSEY. Once on radio, now well-made, animated, fun-packed action tales with inspirational messages. From Focus on the Family. If your store does not carry them, contact Focus on the Family at 1-800-A-Family.

COLBY'S MISSING MEMORY. Maranatha presents this entertaining musical featuring popular songs for kids.

COLOR ME A RAINBOW. A children's series which describes Jesus as Friend, King, Big Brother, God's son and Savior through the use of puppets, music, crafts and Bible verses.

THE EVERLASTING ADVENTURE SERIES. Animated tales to draw kids to the Bible. (Honey Creek)

GERBERT (HSH Educational Media). Animated series aimed at little kids. Biblical principles dealing with several subjects such as peer pressure, love, honesty, etc.

THE GREATEST ADVENTURE. Hanna-Barbera's animated stories about biblical heroes such as Jesus, Moses, David, Noah, Samson and others. Well made for kids—entertaining and educational.

The series now includes The Easter Story, as seen through the eyes of three young visitors from the 20th Century.

THE LION, THE WITCH AND THE WARD-ROBE. (Public Media Video). A 4-star adaptation of the C. S. Lewis classic tale. This is really superb programming for the family, complete with terrific special effects, animation, as well as live action, musical score, and costumes.

A group of children discover a closet that leads to a far-off land called Narnia. The tale is full of Christian analogies and symbolism.

The 174-minute length will take more than one evening to digest, but it serves to open a dialogue between parent and child concerning the sacrifice Jesus made on our behalf. Contact your local Christian bookstore or video shop. If they don't carry this children's masterpiece, ask them to order it.

MCGEE & ME! (Focus on the Family). Look for these well-made animated children's videos at your Christian bookstores.

The producers of these entertaining videos also feature the stories in book form. These are highly recommended as they bring out the fun-loving nature of the cartoon character, McGee, and also develop more fully the spiritual truths each video episode portrays. And besides, they're just plain fun to read!

The first *McGee & Me!* installment, "The Big Lie," has become the number one selling children's video and has received several ecstatic reviews.

Finally, the quality of children's Christian programming has risen to a level where it can not only compete with secular TV programs, but surpass them.

NINTENDO—Bible Adventures for Nintendo by Wisdom Tree. Three adventures in a cartridge where kids help the hero accomplish his mission. "Assisted by scores of direct quotes from the Bible, your adventure will be fun and educational."

> **Noah's Ark**—you help bring in the animals.
> **Save Baby Moses**—you outsmart Pharaoh's soldiers.
> **David & Goliath**—you face the giant along with David.

MUSICAL

COTTON PATCH GOSPEL. This is an excellent musical comedy for teens and adults. The story centers on the Gospel of Matthew, with the settings in modern times—and Jesus being born in Gainesville, Georgia. Great music by the late

Harry Chapin. Truly a joy to watch, and appropriate for any denomination. My highest recommendation.

HIS LAND. A musical journey into the soul of Israel.

THE MUSIC BOX. A 27-minute fantasy/parable about a discouraged assembly-line worker who encounters a chorus of angels. They bequeath him a magical box. Features the inspiring music of the sensational Nightingales.

TEACHING

FACE TO FACE. Tackles tough questions concerning segregation and prejudice in the Christian community. Listen to what the Scriptures say about racism and multi-ethnic relationships. Presented by Inter Varsity Christian Fellowship. For more info about IVCF call (800) 828-2100.

JESUS, THE CHRIST. Realistic dramatization in a 6-part video series on the life of Christ. Presented by Vanguard Video/Family Films.

LOVE IS A DECISION. Gary Smalley. Proven principles to energize your marriage and family (Word).

A MAN CALLED NORMAN. Mike Adkins, a gifted speaker and evangelist, offers you a glimpse of God's heart as he focuses on one of the most profound commandments in the Bible—love your neighbor.

MOLDER OF DREAMS. Guy Doud's heartwarming and humorous presentation gives parents and teachers who mold young people's lives a fresh perspective on their unseen needs. Students will identify with Guy's schooltime experiences and come away with renewed hope for the future.

TWICE PARDONED. Ex-con talks to teens and their parents. Presented by Focus on the Family.

WHERE JESUS WALKED. High-quality visual series depicting the life of Jesus. Ideal for home and church. There are 13 volumes in the series, each 26 minutes in length.

A WINNABLE WAR. Dr. Dobson explains why pornography is addictive, how it affects Christian homes, and what can be done to remove it from our society.

TEENS

FIRE BY NITE. Blaine Bartel reaches thousands of teenagers yearly with crusades, missions, conferences, and his nationwide TV show, "Fire By Nite." Bartel presents a video series featuring interviews with your favorite musical artists along with their latest music videos. Also featured on the videos are skits and a brief message of faith. For more information about this interesting video serious for teens, call (800) 888-7856.

HELL'S BELLS. Reel to Real presents a documentary aiming at youth concerning the secular music industry and how rock and roll affects our society. The film features the music of many top secular groups.

THE TEENAGE Q & A VIDEO SERIES. Josh McDowell and teens discuss topics important to young people, including "How Far is Too Far" and "Questions Boys & Girls Have About Each Other" (Word).

WITHOUT RESERVATION (1989—25 min.). Aimed at the teen market, this story deals with a fatal automobile accident and the six students involved as they find themselves suspended somewhere between heaven and hell. As they view those left behind, each has a different reaction to their fate. It is a sobering story, yet one filled with truth. Well made and very moving. Contact Mars Hill Productions for nearest distributor. Call (800) 866-6479.

CHAPTER V

JOHN WAYNE, THE WESTERN AND YOU

Throughout this book I have ambushed filmmakers for their assiduous use of violence. So where does that leave the western? Often their themes range from greed to revenge, and I have yet to see an audience-pleasing western that didn't contain a shoot-out or two. But the most successful westerns have been so because they were actually morality plays. As with the early horror films, story tellers used the western theme as a good vs. evil parable.

I believe movie-goers find more than that in the endurable western, however. In life, we struggle through daily defeats, often finding ourselves living through unjust circumstances. Perhaps that is the true reason for the popularity of the western and why it is making a comeback. It is, quite simply, a release.

With its thematic style, we experience life as either black or white. There is no grey area. The good guys eventually best the bad guys.

In the book *The Western Films of John Ford* from Citadel Press, author J. A. Place puts it best: "Even when story lines are cliché and predictable, the working out of insoluble tensions and frustrations through fantasy helps to relieve similar tensions in our own lives." Place goes on to say, "...the West represents a pure, natural, fertile wilderness in which the society of man can build a new community based on the cleansing, healing effects of nature."

Recent films aiming to put a new spin on the subject matter such as *Young Guns* and Clint Eastwood's award-winning *Unforgiven*, unfortunately stray from the intent of the western film. In the case of *Unforgiven*, the heros are little more than paid assassins, an element that changes the entire theme of the western genre. But I agree with J.A. Place in that the classic westerns may indeed be a healthy release during these stressful times.

With the western, you need a symbol of strength, self-reliance, fair-play and intolerance toward injustice. John Wayne became that symbol.

Of all the super-stars Hollywood has given birth to, no one has received more criticism for his acting ability than the "Duke." However, I have perceived over the years that Wayne was attacked mainly by those who disagreed with his politics. Coming from a more simplistic time, when social issues were examined differently, John Wayne was never afraid to vocalize his opinions on any subject ranging from the women's movement, to socialistic politics, to the war in Vietnam. Yet, those who worked with him, such as Kirk Douglas, held Duke Wayne in high regard, finding him tolerant of those who professed a more liberal stance on social issues.

I have learned over the years not to try to defend John Wayne. You either love him or you don't. Most critics, however, grudgingly admit that he could, in fact, act. His many low-budgeted oaters and poorly-scripted actioneers may cause some of you to disagree. His fans forgave him for *Jet Pilot*, *Rio Lobo*, *The Conqueror*, etc., because, although they didn't believe the movie, they always believed him. And isn't that how you signify a good actor?

The consummate actress Colleen Dewhurst called him an American phenomenon. I guess that's what he truly was. He transcended being a mere actor. Like Mount Rushmore, he represented qualities we hope to find in ourselves and in our country.

Now, many may feel we shouldn't watch westerns. I respect their views as I am against killing my fellow man, against revenge and against the idea that we can survive as "loners," a common characteristic of the screen cowboy. But I love a good western. For me, they are not just a release of hostile tensions toward the wrongs of this world but, like jazz music or hamburgers, the western is uniquely American, and truly fun.

Here is a list of my favorite horse-operas.

GUNFIGHT AT THE O.K. CORRAL (1957). Burt Lancaster, Kirk Douglas. Another relating of the O.K. Corral, helped along by bravado performances and an unforgettable score by Dimitri Tiomkin. (Music is an essential element to the success of the western, as evidenced by *The Magnificent Seven*. . .)

HOW THE WEST WAS WON (1962). This three-hour extravaganza was filmed using the Cinerama process (with three cameras) and starred everybody in Hollywood! With Spencer Tracy serving as narrator, it tells of the building of the west, maybe not as it was, but certainly the way it should have been.

THE MAGNIFICENT SEVEN (1960). Yul Brynner, Steve McQueen, Eli Wallach. Derived from the Kurosawa *Eastern*, about seven gunmen defending a poor Mexican village from bandits. Every part perfectly cast and Elmer Bernstein's music is outstanding. Replete with symbolism.

THE MAN WHO SHOT LIBERTY VALANCE (1962). John Wayne, James Stewart, Lee Marvin. Concentrating more on character than outdoor action, John Ford tells the story of a rancher who allows a dude to think he has killed the town villain, thereby using the incident as a stepping stone to a political career.

MY DARLING CLEMENTINE (1946). Henry Fonda, Victor Mature, Walter Brennan. Full of John Ford details and the descriptive photography of Joseph P. MacDonald, this is a superb telling of the legend of Wyatt Earp and the O.K. Corral.

RIDE THE HIGH COUNTRY (1962). Randolph Scott, Joel McCrea. A poignant film signaling the end of the western genre with two old pros playing aged gunslingers guarding a gold shipment. A literate script and breathtaking scenery make this a must-see for western enthusiasts.

RIO BRAVO. John Wayne, Dean Martin. The sheriff stands against a corrupt land baron aided by only two deputies, one a drunk, the other a cripple. By the early '50s, Wayne was already the quintessential folk hero, but 1959's *Rio Bravo* served to describe the Wayne mystique. The stance, the swagger, the drawl were all well-defined in this leisurely played out western tale. The Duke was now a western icon.

THE SEARCHERS (1956). John Wayne, Jeffrey Hunter, Natalie Wood. Considered by many critics to be one of the finest films ever, it tells the story of Ethan Edwards returning home several years after the Civil War. Soon his brother's family is murdered by a Comanche raiding party who kidnap his young niece (played as a little girl by Natalie's sister Lana). Years later, Wayne's character rightly fears the girl is now one of the chief's wives. Will the Injun-hating Ethan kill her rather than see her become a "squaw?" In this reviewer's opinion, this is John Ford's most complex western and certainly the most majestic visually. The perfect western. A perfect movie.

SHANE (1953). Alan Ladd. A perfect morality play

set in the Old West. Great cinematography, sound, score and textbook editing highlight one of the best westerns ever made.

THREE GODFATHERS (1948). John Wayne, Pedro Armendariz, Harry Carey, Jr. Three outlaws, running from a posse, come across a dying woman and her newborn baby. The symbolism between the Christ-child and this new foundling has a redemptive effect on the three bandits. Sincere performances, beautiful cinematography and the skillful direction of John Ford highlight this insightful western.

TRUE GRIT (1969). John Wayne, Kim Darby, Glen Campbell, Robert Duvall. Hampered only by Campbell's unskilled acting, *True Grit* stands tall as rousing western fare. Duke's rugged, one-eyed Rooster Cogburn was possibly his most energetic, definitive performance and worthy of that year's Best Actor Oscar.

And, of course, there is John Ford's trilogy, *Fort Apache* (1948), *She Wore a Yellow Ribbon* (1949), and *Rio Grande* (1950), each starring John Wayne and Ford's stock company, which consisted of some of the finest supporting actors known to the silver screen. Each a powerful character study enhanced by the awesome Monument Valley, and some of the finest horsemanship ever photographed.

CHAPTER VI

COMMENTS FROM MEDIA PERSON-ALITIES

Macdonald Carey, the perennial Dr. Tom Horton of *Days of Our Lives*, has had quite a history in Hollywoodland—a formitable leading man of the '40s and '50s in such vehicles as Alfred Hitchcock's *Shadow of a Doubt* and John Farrow's *Wake Island*.

He has worked on the stage, in radio, films, and besides his 28-year stint on *Days*, Mr. Carey appeared in two other series, *Dr. Christian* (1956) and *Lock-Up* ('59-'61).

Mac's favorite role in a western was in the 1956 *Stranger at My Door*, about a minister trying to reform an outlaw. Not yet on video, it can be found on the late, late show. Definitely worth VCRing.

Concerned with the direction young filmmakers are taking the medium, Mr. Carey has this to say:

> "It's too bad pictures don't return to the simplicity they once had. They were essentially morality plays peopled by human beings, not machines.

> "And comedians got their laughs without resorting to four-letter words.

> "And all in all, the message of the film was in your heart rather than in your face."

Michael Medved is a perceptive film critic, a provocative writer, and one of the very few in his line of work willing to put his career in jeopardy for his beliefs. His book *Hollywood vs. America* (due out in paperback in August 1993) is a persuasive indictment containing chapters dealing with "The Attack on Religion," "The Assault on the Family," "The Infatuation with Foul Language," and "America Bashing."

Cohost of PBS's "Sneak Previews," Medved has this to say:

> "What ails today's films has nothing to do with the prowess or professionalism

of the filmmakers. The true sickness is in the soul."[2]

Hollywood vs. America is the most important book you can own concerning the subject of the direction Hollywood is leading our society and what we can do about it. He's factual, respectful, and most insightful.

Pat Boone, renown as a pop singer of the '50s, also appeared in several movies, including *Bernardine* (1957), *April Love* (1957), *Journey to the Center of the Earth* (1959), *State Fair* (1962), *Goodbye Charlie* (1964), *The Greatest Story Ever Told* (1965), *The Perils of Pauline* (1967), and *The Cross and the Switchblade* (1972).

But taking a stand for his religious beliefs probably cost Boone a lifelong career as a movie star. His stand for decency and family values, however, has gained him a legion of respectful fans.

> "Movies today, and indeed almost all that calls itself entertainment, have by and large become nothing more than moral pollution.

> "We're concerned about 'acid rain' and other adverse influences on our physical environment, and well we should be. But far worse, in my opinion, is the corrosive and cancerous invasion on our moral and spiritual senses of today's movies, theatre and television and cable varieties included. Anything and everything that used to be 'taboo,' forbidden in the name of decency and even good taste, is rushed to our screens and into our living rooms in rich color, stereophonic sound and multi-million-dollar production. Rampant sex, gross violence, filthy obscenity, sacrilege, perversion and every kind of human indecency is spewed out in our faces, and then commended by critics and awarded by the industries. Oscar-winning actors and actresses drop their clothes, spout obscenities and simulate every sexual act known to man, and collect big paychecks.

> "The first chapter of Romans describes all of this, and the most frightening promise is that 'God gave them over to a reprobate mind' to do every kind of

2 Michael Medved, *Hollywood vs. America* (Harper Collins/Zondervon), p. 11.

evil.

"This is that day, and the entertainment industry is right in the thick of it, moving it briskly along. The cash register provides the macabre music to this dance of death—and concerned parents *must* erect the 'safe houses' for themselves and their children against the tide."

Frank Capra, the celebrated film director, gave us countless masterpieces, including *It Happened One Night, Mr. Deeds Goes to Town, Lost Horizon, Meet John Doe, Mr. Smith Goes to Washington*, and perhaps the greatest of all, *It's a Wonderful Life.*

"Movies should be a positive expression that there is hope, love, mercy, justice and charity...It is the filmmaker's responsibility to emphasize the positive qualities of humanity by showing the triumph of the individual over adversities."[3]

John Clemens, News Director, USA Radio Network:

"There is no way we will ever be able to ascertain the enormity of the detrimental influence the entertainment industry has had on our society.

"Yes, we can count the broken lives and the lifeless bodies, but what about the 'rivers' of tears that have been shed for those who have been lost.

"Today, in America, gratuitous violence is disguised as 'action' or 'adult' and the crime rate has skyrocketed. There can be very little doubt left in anyone's mind about the correlation between violence and the increased amount of aggressiveness in our children.

"The 'neighborhood' of our youth is very different from today. The 'neighborhood' of today is the VCR and the cable TV selector box. The 'boogie man' of our imagination of yesterday is alive today and awaits its next victim."

---

[3] Charles Camplin, "Frank Capra's Wonderful Life," *Los Angeles Times*, September 5, 1992, p. F1.

CHAPTER VIII

HOW YOU CAN HAVE A POSITIVE INFLUENCE ON HOLLYWOOD

In a land controlled by media, isn't it sad how many people don't communicate?

Hollywood listens and responds to viewers. Each letter is like hearing from a thousand people, which means yours does count. So why aren't our views being expressed in the movies? Perhaps it's because *we're* not communicating.

Might I suggest that when corresponding with members of the motion picture or television industries, you keep your letters precise, to the point and, most of all, short! Often in our frustration we react with anger and wordiness. Very seldom does this tactic present us in our best light.

Simply let them know what you like, what you don't like, and why. Keep it to a couple of paragraphs.

Would you really like to have an influence on the movie capitol? PRAY over that letter before writing it. *You* can't change anyone's heart, but the Holy Spirit can.

Will a change really occur?

For 30 years we've been warned to clean up our planet. Finally we are taking responsibility and a difference is being seen. With an informed commitment we can also affect the artistic community. The crucial word here is **responsibility.**

Listed are many of the studios, networks and cable companies. Let them know how you feel. It's time the silent majority spoke up.

I have also included two letters—neither is an example of great prose, but merely an honest expression of my feelings concerning the direction the media is taking our society.

Of course, I'm not suggesting that letter-writing campaigns are the solution to this complex problem, but I do feel the answer is simple in definition.

In this reviewer's humble opinion, changes will

occur when we take *responsibility*. (1) Communicate with the industry. (2) Be careful what you support. And (3) make your children understand the importance of traditional values and point out Hollywood's lack of regard for those values. It really could be that simple.

Most of us still foolishly consider the television or movie theater to be a babysitter or anesthetic. If, indeed, the media is contributing to the violence and lack of morality in our society, then maybe we shouldn't continue to ignore its power.

Probably the most effective way to get your views across would be to approach the local affiliates. You'll find them listed in your phone book.

COLUMBIA PICTURES, 10202 W. Washington, Culver City, CA 90222, (310) 280-8000.

WALT DISNEY COMPANY, 500 S. Buena Vista St., Burbank, CA 91521, (818) 840-1000.

MCA/UNIVERSAL PICTURES, 100 Universal City Plaza, Universal City, CA 91608, (818) 777-1000.

NEW WORLD PICTURES, 1440 S. Sepulveda Blvd., Los Angeles, CA 90025, (310) 444-8100.

PARAMOUNT PICTURES, 5555 Melrose Avenue, Los Angeles, CA 90038, (310) 956-5000.

TWENTIETH CENTURY-FOX, 10201 W. Pico Blvd., Los Angeles, CA 90035, (310) 277-2211.

UNITED ARTISTS, 450 N. Roxbury Drive, Beverly Hills, CA 90210.

WARNER BROTHERS, 4000 Warner Blvd., Burbank, CA 91522, (818) 954-6000.

CROWN INTERNATIONAL PICTURES, 8701 Wilshire Boulevard, Beverly Hills, CA 90211, (310) 657-6700.

THE SAMUEL GOLDWYN COMPANY, 10203 Santa Monica Blvd., Los Angeles, CA 90067, (310) 552-2255.

HEMDALE FILM CORPORATION, 7966 Beverly Blvd., Los Angeles, CA 90048, (213) 966-3700.

ISLAND PICTURES, 9000 Sunset Boulevard, Los Angeles, CA 90069, (310) 276-4500.

KINGS ROAD ENTERTAINMENT, 1901 Ave. of the Stars, Suite 605, Los Angeles, CA 90067, (310) 552-0057.

CASTLE HILL PICTURES, 153 Waverly Place, New York, NY 10014, (212) 888-0080.

LORIMAR-TELEPICTURES, 3970 Overland Avenue, Culver City, CA 90230, (213) 202-2000, Merv Adelson, Chairman.

LUCASFILM, P O Box 2009, San Rafael, CA 94902, (415) 457-5282, George Lucas, Chairman.

MIRAMAX FILMS, 18 East 48th Street, New York, NY 10017, (212) 941-3800.

NEW LINE CINEMA, 575 Eighth Avenue, 16th Floor, New York, NY 10018, (212) 239-8880.

ORION PICTURES, 1875 Century Park East, Suite 300, Los Angeles, CA 90067, Arthur Krim, Chairman.

RASTAR PRODUCTIONS, Columbia Plaza West, Burbank, CA 91505, (818) 954-2400, Ray Stark, Chairman.

TOUCHSTONE PICTURES, Walt Disney Company, 500 S. Buena Vista St., Burbank, CA 91521.

UNIVERSAL PICTURES, 100 Universal City, Universal City, CA 91608, (818) 777-1000, Tom Pollack, President.

VESTRON, 1011 High Ridge Rd., Stamford, CT 06907.

THE ZANUCK/BROWN COMPANY, 202 N. Canon Drive, Beverly Hills, CA 90210, (310) 274-5929, Richard Zanuck, President.

MGM, 10000 W. Washington Blvd., Culver City, CA 90232, (213) 280-6000.

ZOETROPE STUDIOS, 916 Kearny Street, San Francisco, CA 94133, (415) 788-7500, Francis Ford Coppola, President.

CINEMAX, 1100 Ave. of the Americas, New York, NY 10036, (212) 512-1000.

CNBC, 2200 Fletcher Ave., Ft. Lee, NJ 07024, (201) 585-2622.

CNN, One CNN Center, P O Box 105366, Atlanta, GA 30348.

DISNEY CHANNEL, 3800 W. Alameda Ave., Burbank, CA 91505, (818) 569-7500.

ETERNAL WORD TV/CATHOLIC, 5817 Old Leeds Rd., Birmingham, AL 35210, (205) 956-9537.

THE FAMILY CHANNEL, 1000 Centerville Turnpike, Virginia Beach, VA 23463, (804) 523-7301.

HBO, 1100 Ave. of the Americas, New York, NY 10036, (212) 512-1000.

LIFETIME, Lifetime Astoria Studios, 36-12 35th Ave.,

Astoria, NY 11106, (718) 482-4000.

MOVIE CHANNEL, 1633 Broadway, New York, NY 10019, (212) 708-1600.

MTV, 1515 Broadway, New York, NY 10036.

NASHVILLE, 2806 Opryland Drive, Nashville, TN 37214, (615) 889-6840.

NICKELODEON, 1515 Broadway, New York, NY 10036.

SHOWTIME, 1633 Broadway, New York, NY 10019, (212) 708-1600.

TBS, P O Box 105366, Atlanta, GA 30348.

TNT, 1515 Broadway, New York, NY 10036.

USA, 1230 Ave. of the Americas, New York, NY 10020, (212) 408-9100.

WGN, 3801 S. Sheridan Road, Tulsa, OK 74145.

ABC, Attention Broadcast Standards, 77 West 66th Street, New York, NY 10023.

CBS, Attention Broadcast Standards, 51 West 52nd Street, New York, NY 10019.

FOX BROADCASTING, P O Box 900, Beverly Hills, CA 90213.

NBC, Attention Broadcast Standards, 30 Rockefeller Plaza, New York, NY 10112.

PBS, 1320 Braddock Place, Alexandria, VA 22314-1698.

AMERICAN MOVIE CLASSICS, 150 Crossways Park West, Woodbury, NY 11797.

FEDERAL COMMUNICATIONS COMMISSION, 1919 M Street, NW, Washington, DC 20554, (202) 632-7117.

Arts & Entertainment Network, 235 E. 45th St., New York, NY 10017.

May 10, 1990

Linda Bloodworth-Thomason, Producer
Designing Women
CBS
7800 Beverly Blvd.
Los Angeles, CA 90036

Dear Ms. Thomason:

I just wanted to thank you for your depiction of a Christian pastor on your May 7, 1990 airing of *Designing Women*.

It was refreshing to see a minister, a Christian man, presented as a real person, who just happens to believe in and respect
God. So often, TV's "religious" characters are portrayed as
either fanatics or hypocrites.

The episode was both funny and moving and you won me
over as a regular viewer. Perhaps if more producers would
be fair in their presentation of Believers, they would find the
Christian community a more receptive audience.

Sincerely,

Phil Boatwright
Editor
The Movie Reporter

The following letter to the editor ran in the *Los Angeles
Times* "Calendar" section in response to an article by TV
producer Steven Bochco (*Hill Street Blues, L.A. Law, Cop
Rock*), who stated that television would be better off without
censors.

One of Bochco's solutions to the dwindling
reception of network programming is to do away
with censors. How many really believe that the
quality would go up if that were done?

Would we get more shows like *Masterpiece
Theatre* or *Hill Street Blues*? No, we'd just get
more profane language, more violence and more
exploitative sex. And definitely more "politically
correct" thinking from the industry's rather liberal
sect. Excuse me, but don't we already have all that
in our movie theaters? And look where that's
taking us.

The answer to improving the ratings—improve
the material. *Cop Rock* indeed!

Phil Boatwright

Thousand Oaks

CHAPTER VIII

THE AUTHOR'S FAVORITES

The following chapter contains a list of *my* favorite movies. Since we each have our own opinion as to which movie ranks as best of all time, I choose not to debate the qualifications of *Gone With The Wind*, *Citizen Kane* or *Potemkin* as the pinnacle of filmmaking. I would rather focus on films that have touched me in a personal way. Motion pictures, like fine paintings, can be works of art. When you discover great ones, they should be shared.

Among these, some contain a few expletives or situations not in keeping with the Christian concept. So why have I included them? Well, it's like looking at a glass of water and seeing it either half empty or half full. Does the profundity eclipse the profanity, so to speak. These films have moved me or taught me about life and the need for a spiritual development. Please keep in mind that this book is *not* about films with no "bad" words. It *is* about movies that uplift, entertain or exemplify, without pummeling your senses with negative images or language.

Sometimes we are *made aware* by looking at a life that has everything *but* a spiritual development. It's a reminder to us that no one is ever completely satisfied without a place in the heart for God.

I stand by each of these motion pictures as 4-star works of art, but I suggest you use discernment when deciding which films you should view. Note has been made of the three or four films on my list containing any bad language or adult subject matter. I'd rather you pass on them if you are offended by the presence of even one or two obscene words. As for me, I was moved, entertained, or challenged by each video listed here.

BABETTE'S FEAST (1987). Based on a short story by Isak Dinessen about two sisters in a small Danish town who take in a homeless woman as their servant. A beautiful story of devotion and sacrifice urging us not to hide behind our religion, but to put it into action. Winner of the Best Foreign Film of that year and should not be missed. More like viewing a fine old painting or enjoying a sumptuous meal, it is a remarkable example American filmmakers could take a lesson from. Most video stores carry this one in the foreign film section. (Easy to read subtitles.)

THE BEST YEARS OF OUR LIVES (1946). Fredric March (one of the screen's best actors), Myrna Loy and an all-star cast tell a sensitive story of returning WWII service men and how they must adapt to civilian life. This seven-Oscar winner rests comfortably among the ten best films of all time!

Noteworthy Facts:

- Real-life disabled veteran Harold Russell won two Oscars for this film—as Best Supporting Actor and a special award for "bringing hope and courage to his fellow veterans."

CASABLANCA (1942). Humphrey Bogart, Ingrid Bergman. I have always considered *Citizen Kane* the one flawless film, but after a recent viewing of Rick & Elsa's great love story, I've capitulated—*Casablanca* truly reigns as the greatest motion picture of all time. (I'm a man of definite opinions as you have gathered.) But I *cannot* find a false or ineffective camera angle, line or performance in the entire production. Love, honor and patriotism prevail.

Noteworthy Facts:

- George Raft was considered for the lead.
- The song "As Time Goes By" was almost cut from the film.
- Winner of Best Picture, Screenplay and Director Oscars, 1943.

COTTON PATCH GOSPEL (1988). A musical comedy/drama placing the Gospel of Matthew in modern-day Georgia. Funny, moving, inspirational. Contact your local Christian bookstore. If not in stock, ask them to order it. (Distributed by The Bridgestone Production Group.) One of the most inspiring treatments of the New Testament I've seen on video. Effective for both teens and adults. My highest recommendation.

DR. STRANGELOVE, OR HOW I LEARNED TO STOP WORRYING AND LOVE THE BOMB (1964). Peter Sellers, George C. Scott. Definitely adult subject matter here, but the powerful "stupidity of war" theme and outstanding dark comedic performances, including Sellers, Scott, Keenan Wynn and Sterling Hayden, make this valid movie fare.

THE GREAT RACE (1965). Rated G. A comic spoof of old-time melodramas, with Jack Lemmon very funny as the villainous Professor Fate, Tony Curtis stalwart as the Great Leslie, and Natalie Wood luminous as...well, as Natalie Wood.

GUESS WHO'S COMING TO DINNER (1967). Spencer Tracy, Katharine Hepburn, Sidney Poitier. The subject, interracial marriage, is defended by some, disapproved by others. Some say it's difficult enough finding love in this world—why should race be the eliminating factor? My views are probably not that difficult to assess, but that's not our purpose here. Politics aside, race relations aside, *Dinner* has three outstanding performances from three of my favorite actors. Still, as I have always maintained, a great performance is not reason enough for seeing a movie. What's being said and how it's being said should be a factor in choosing a video nowadays. *Guess Who's Coming To Dinner* discusses race relations, a relevant subject, and does so without abusing the viewer with hostile language or explicit sexual situations. No matter how you rule concerning interracial couplings, director Stanley Kramer makes us all a little more sensitive to the people dealing intimately with this situation. Caution: there are a few expletives.

Noteworthy Facts:

- Tracy and Hepburn's ninth and last film, as Tracy died of heart disease just a few days after filming was completed.

HANNA AND HER SISTERS (1986). Woody Allen, Michael Caine, Mia Farrow, Barbara Hershey. I am aware many would be offended by the few profanities and adult situations in this film; therefore, I'm not recommending it. I simply list *Hanna* for its creative treatment of Woody's continued search for the meaning of life. Remember, I am a film historian, I don't judge a film to be quality just because it has no swear words. *Hanna and Her Sisters* is great filmmaking—funny and insightful. In this work, he lampoons his own intellectualism and reluctantly admits that perhaps chaos doesn't rule. Leaving the theater, I felt grateful I had something Hannah and her sisters were searching for, a relationship with God through Jesus Christ.

Noteworthy Facts:

- Lloyd Nolan's last picture.
- The Marx Brothers' film clip used near the end came from *Duck Soup*.
- Both Dianne Wiest and Michael Caine won Oscars in the Best Supporting category.

IT'S A MAD, MAD, MAD, MAD WORLD (1963). All-star cast includes Spencer Tracy, Milton Berle, Sid Caesar, Buddy Hackett, Ethel Merman, Mickey Rooney...oh, heck, it stars every major comic from the '30s to the '60s! A non-stop laugh-a-thon as a group of motorists learn of a fortune buried 200 miles away. Rated G and certainly one of the funniest movies ever made. Now available in a wide-screen format, including newly restored sequences and interviews with the director and several of the cast members.

JAWS (1975). Richard Dreyfuss, Robert Shaw. When this film was first released, no one left the theater for popcorn. They were glued to their seats with anticipation. A frightening, entertaining morality play about a shark who terrorizes a resort community. Unfortunately, it contains several unnecessary profanities and obscenities, so beware if you decide to rent it. Pass on the sequels; the magic died with the first Great White.

LAWRENCE OF ARABIA (1962). Peter O'Toole. Speaking of film experiences, *Lawrence of Arabia* is another that must be viewed on the big screen to be totally appreciated. I first saw this Best Picture of 1962 on TV and was disappointed. Years later I saw the restored version in a Los Angeles theater and was knocked out. Like Hitchcock, Director David Lean is very visual. His work has to be seen on the big screen to capture all he's saying. (Even the letter-boxed laser disc is disappointing.) My advice: Look for *Lawrence* at revival houses or to be re-released every ten years or so. This one's too great to be imprisoned on television.

THE MALTESE FALCON (1941). There's never been a more sardonic detective than Sam Spade or a more intriguing detective film noire than *The Maltese Falcon*. Made previously, this is one of the few remakes that outshines the original. Directed by John Huston and superbly cast with Humphrey Bogart, Peter Lorrie, Sydney Greenstreet and Elisha Cook, Jr. Often referred to as the definitive private eye story, it may seem cliched now as every ingredient making this the best of its genre has been unremarkably reproduced by many a filmmaker. The only negative I found in this atmospheric classic was the casting of Mary Astor, who was by then too old for the part and far from the alluring seductress the character called for. Lauren Bacall would have been a perfect choice. Unfortunately, Ms. Bacall was only about sixteen at the time. "Baby" wouldn't be discovered until three years later when Hollywood had the good sense to team her with Bogey in *To Have and Have Not*.

MOTHER TERESA (1987). Petrie Productions. In a time when the media is focusing on the follies of some TV evangelists, here's a documentary about a group of women putting Christ's teachings into practice. A life-changing film about an order of nuns who serve mankind. Here is evidence that if we treated others the way we wish to be treated, we would erase starvation, greed and all other evils from the face of the earth.

MR. SMITH GOES TO WASHINGTON (1939). Jimmy Stewart reminds us what American politicians should aspire to. This really is a fabulous movie. Come to think of it, have you ever known anyone who didn't like Jimmy Stewart?!

<u>Noteworthy Facts:</u>

- Nominated for Best Picture Oscar in 1939. Other contenders that year: *Dark Victory, Gone with The Wind, Goodbye, Mr. Chips, Love Affair, Ninotchka, Of Mice and Men, Stagecoach, The Wizard of Oz, Wuthering Heights.* Do you know the winner? It was a tough choice that year, which presented these and many other great films, making 1939 Hollywood's Golden Year, providing more classics than any other year in cinema history. The Oscar winner: *Gone With The Wind.*

MY FAIR LADY (1964). Rex Harrison, Audrey Hepburn. Another exception to the Hollywood musical. This eight-Oscar winner will enchant you with its ingratiating performances and memorable show-stoppers ("The Rain in Spain," "I've Grown Accustomed To Her Face," and "Get Me To The Church On Time").

Noteworthy Facts:

- It's reported that upon being offered the part of Professor Henry Higgins, Cary Grant refused by saying, "If you don't get Rex Harrison for the part, I won't even go see the film."
- Julie Andrews had played the part of Eliza Doolittle on stage, but lost out to Audrey Hepburn for the film as Ms. Hepburn was considered more "bankable." Later that year, Andrews won an Oscar for *Mary Poppins*. Many considered it a consolation prize.

NETWORK (1976). William Holden, Robert Duvall, Peter Finch, Faye Dunaway. Paddy Chayefsky left us with many thoughts that have stuck a chord in our society. ("I'm mad as hell, and I'm not going to take it anymore.") The film is full of insights not just about the television industry, but our society as well. Due to the rough language throughout and an adulterous affair (which I believe the film could have done without), I cannot recommend this film for general viewing. But the film evidenced that all the money, power or sexual fulfillment would still leave you unsatisfied. Something was missing. I believe that to be character, or perhaps a spiritual enlightenment. Obviously, you don't need to see a film like this in order to be grateful to God for your relationship through Jesus, but that's what it did for me.

Noteworthy Facts:

- Peter Finch was the first performer to win an Academy Award posthumously. In my opinion, William Holden gave the best performance in the film.

ON THE BEACH (1959). Gregory Peck, Ava Gardner, Fred Astaire (in a fine dramatic role). Adroit script about survivors of nuclear war awaiting the end of the world. This film is a terrific example of adult subject matter, including romance, effectively handled with discretion.

ON THE WATERFRONT (1954). Marlon Brando, Eva Marie Saint, Rod Steiger. Winner of eight Academy Awards, dealing with New York's crime-ridden harbor docks. Another excellent example of romance, emotional stress and vice masterfully told without the language and brutality associated with today's movies.

PATTON (1970). George C. Scott. One of the best war/anti-war films ever made. Truly a textbook example of outstanding filmmaking. A faithful account of one of the most colorful and controversial warriors of all time. Caution: Patton used colorful language, and so does the movie. However, the expletives are not used for shock value, but rather as a development of this man's character. After all, that's how Patton spoke. Patton was a complex man: on one hand a foul-mouthed eccentric, on the other, a soft-spoken connoisseur who swore allegiance to God as well as country. Although I would be at odds with many of his religious views (he believed in reincarnation), still I have high regard for anyone professing a respect for God.

Noteworthy Facts:

- Richard Nixon claims *Patton* to be his favorite movie.
- The title role was offered to Robert Mitchum, Rod Steiger, and Burt Lancaster, among others, before Scott accepted what would become his most famous role.
- George C. Scott refused his Best Actor Oscar.

THE QUIET MAN (1952). John Wayne, Maureen O'Hara. Now, I'm an unabashed John Wayne fan. A dangerous statement if you are desiring to be taken seriously as a film reviewer. However, most film historians grudgingly accept the Duke as one of the strongest personas ever to appear on celluloid. Some even take umbrage to the pronouncement that he could not act. (View *The Searchers, The Cowboys, The Shootist, True Grit, The Sands of Iwo Jima* or *She Wore a Yellow Ribbon*, then tell me he couldn't act.) From my research over the years, I've discovered John Wayne *was* John Wayne. Bigger than life with a Mount Rushmore identity, Wayne was brave, tough, generous and patriotic. Even political foes like Jack Lemmon and Kirk Douglas stand in awe of what he was and what he stood for. True, no one has made more needless films (*Rio Lobo, The Conqueror, Jet Pilot*), but on the other hand, few have given us any more entertaining pictures than *The Quiet Man*. In it Wayne is indomitable in dealing with Victor McLaglen, humorous with Barry Fitzgerald, and tender with one of the most beautiful women on the movie screen, Maureen O'Hara. John Ford won a deserving Best Director Oscar for this production of a man returning to his roots and discovering that love with an Irish redhead can be as rocky and beautiful as Ireland itself. A loving, sentimental look at the Ireland we all wish existed. Great music, cinematography and story make this one of the Duke's best. Romance, humor and one of the longest fight scenes ever filmed!

REAR WINDOW (1954). James Stewart and perhaps the most regal actress of all time, Grace Kelly. Directed by Alfred Hitchcock, it is an outstanding suspense thriller with equal ingredients of romance and humor. A macabre tale of voyeurism and murder as a photographer is convinced that a neighbor did in his own wife.

SHANE (1953). Alan Ladd. A perfect morality play set in the Old West. Great cinematography, sound, score, and textbook editing highlight one of the best westerns ever made.

THAT'S ENTERTAINMENT, Parts 1 and 2. (1974, 1976). The perfect musicals for those of us who love the artistry of MGM's stable of stars yet hate the corny story lines that so often accompanied the '30s and '40s musical comedies. No silly scenarios here, just Astaire, Rogers and about a hundred other luminaries doing what they do best.

TO KILL A MOCKINGBIRD (1962). Gregory Peck. Horton Foote's winning screenplay of the Harper Lee novel about rural life, justice, honor and bigotry as seen through the eyes of a nine-year-old girl. A beautifully photographed black-and-white movie with a haunting score by Elmer Bernstein. Peck has never been better. Other Horton Foote screenplays paying tribute to old-fashioned ethics: *Tender Mercies, The Trip To Bountiful.*

Noteworthy Facts:

- Rock Hudson wanted the part of Atticus Finch.
- Robert Duvall made his big screen debut as Boo Radley.
- Actress Kim Stanley narrated the film.
- Oscars went to Peck, Horton Foote, and to Oliver Emert for Art Direction and Set Decoration. The film lost out to *Lawrence of Arabia.*

WEST SIDE STORY (1961). Natalie Wood. I am not a big fan of musicals, let alone ones that spotlight dancing gang members, but *West Side Story* transcends the typical Hollywood musical. Not only is every scene filled with artistry, but every frame. You could pause the VCR anywhere in this film and come up with a lasting image. However, if you have the opportunity to see this one in a movie theater, that's the way to go. Viewing on TV with commercials is similar to sacrilege! Based on Shakespeare's tragic Romeo and Juliet, now set in early-1960s New York barrios, Robert Wise, Jerome Robbins, Leonard Bernstein, Stephen Sondheim and the lovely Natalie Wood have turned it into one of the finest film experiences you'll ever have.

Noteworthy Facts:

- John Astin (later Gomez on "The Addams Family") made his screen debut.
- Marni Nixon dubbed Natalie Wood's singing as she did earlier for Deborah Kerr in *The King and I*, and later for Audrey Hepburn in *My Fair Lady*.

Well, I could go on and on, but we'll leave some for Volume 2!

Have a favorite film? Let me know. If I haven't seen it yet, I'll be sure to look for it. If it fits our guidelines (movies that uplift, exemplify, entertain or teach without abusive language, sexual situations or extreme violence), we'll run it in *The Movie Reporter Newsletter*.

CHAPTER IX

SUBSCRIPTION CARD FOR THE MOVIE REPORTER NEWSLETTER

The Movie Reporter is taking a stand against profanity, extreme violence and exploitive sexual situations in the movies by informing you of the content of movies and presenting articles on how we can have a positive influence on the media.

For only $15.00 a year (limited offer), we will update this book with our monthly newsletter. Included in the periodical will be the synopsis and content of newly released movies and their alternatives, new films for kids (that you'll enjoy as well), and inspirational and secular movies for each member of the family. Our motto is: "Know Before You Go." Stay informed. Subscribe to *The Movie Reporter Newsletter*. Makes a great gift for friends, family, or associates at work. Easy to read, taking just a few minutes to peruse, yet presenting details of over 50 theatrical, TV and video movies each month.

Mail your check payable to Central Christian Publications, P.O. Box 7178, Thousand Oaks, CA 91359.

The Movie Reporter
P O Box 7178
Thousand Oaks, CA 91359

Subscription price $15.00 per year (limited offer). Make check payable to **Central Christian Publications.**

Please print name and address.

Name:

Address:

About the Author

Phil Boatwright is vice-president of Central Christian Publications and editor of *The Movie Reporter Newsletter*. Articles about Hollywood from a family perspective by Mr. Boatwright are also featured in newspapers and magazines across the country. He has also reviewed for the U.S.A. Radio Network.

His background includes writing for motion pictures and the theater, creating Christian TV News (a monthly periodical focusing on the Christian TV networks) and acting in several films and in over 60 plays. Recently, he was featured on NBC's daytime soap opera, "Generations."

Phil Boatwright, a dedicated Christian and film historian, is available for speaking engagements, presenting effective suggestions on how the Christian community can have a positive influence on the film industry. For more information about his successful seminar, write to Central Christian Publications, P.O. Box 7178, Thousand Oaks, CA 91359.

Didn't find your favorite film listed here? Well, that's because I'm saving it for Volume 2. See you then!

INDEX